(THE TWO-FIFTY)

the **250**

Evangelism Ideas For Your Campus

"The250, Evangelism Ideas for Your Campus"
©2003 WSN Press, Campus Crusade for Christ Inc.
All rights reserved. No part of this publication may be
reproduced, stored in a retrieval system, or transmitted,
in any form or by any means, electronic, mechanical,
photocopying, recording or otherwise, without the
prior permission of WSN Press.

WSN Press is the publishing division of Campus Crusade
for Christ's Campus Ministry.

ISBN: 1-57334-059-6

Design & Production
Innovation Center for Technology, ICT2003084

Illustrations
Daniela S. Byers

COMMENTS/CORRECTIONS/ADDITIONS
If you have any comments, corrections or additions—
please send them to:

Campus Communications
100 Lake Hart Drive 2500
Orlando, Florida 32832

If you know of any innovative or creative ways to reach
college students or know of any stories that you'd like
included in a subsequent edition of this book, please
submit your idea in an e-mail to **stories@uscm.org**

*TABLE of Contents

(the250)

a safe website to send unbelievers to

what CCC student leaders and staff say:

"Our goal is to reach every student. And it's just been the most valuable tool in doing that."

"All you have to do is make students aware of the website, and thousands of students go to it."

"When you can't answer all the questions that someone might have when you're sharing your faith, refer them to this website. It's a vast resource for answering their real questions."

"I wouldn't hesitate to refer my most skeptical and critical friends here —people I've really invested in and wouldn't want to be put off by some cheezy Christianese site. We've done well here."

for free promotional materials:
www.ESCmedia.org

EveryStudent.com

 # Foreword

As a ministry, Campus Crusade for Christ has been called by God to a great task - helping fulfill the Great Commission in this generation. Our motivation for so great an enterprise, and really our life's purpose, is the glory of God. We have seen lives changed, including our own, when His name is lifted up and we know that the ends of the earth need that same transformation. In the campus ministry, we believe that a vital part of seeing the world reached is seeing each and every college student in the world reached with the life-saving and life-giving message of Jesus.

Because the task is great and the significance is priceless, we have chosen to embrace the apostle Paul's vision in 1 Corinthians 9:22, *"I have become all things to all men so that by all possible means I might save some."*

Our individual response to that vision is to live faith-saturated lives and to believe Him for the souls of lost college students everywhere. It means taking risks and moving out into the unknown and the uncomfortable. It means continually learning and growing. Our response in our ministries is to do the same, to take risks, to learn and grow, and to trust the Lord in ever-increasing dependence and faith.

You hold in your hands a visible demonstration of that conviction. Creative, effective and cutting-edge ideas have been compiled from some 170 of our Campus Crusade movements around the country. Each strategy or idea represents both innovation and faith in a God who pursues the lost by all means.

As we trust God together for the future, for every student having the opportunity to know Jesus, may our own faith be expanded, may our lives more closely resemble our Savior, and may God be glorified as many come to know Him.

Thank you for being a part of God's work in the lives of today's students.

Mark and Kristi Gauthier

U.S. Campus Ministry ✶ National Director

SIMPLE IDEAS FOR
A COMPLEX WORLD

Inspiring new ways to face today's changing culture

Introduction

Imagine gathering with Christian leaders from campus ministries around the nation to share the wealth of new evangelism ideas and initiatives in reaching students. Your mind is engaged as you consider your plans for the future. Your creativity is sparked as you consider new approaches that are out of the box you've operated in. Your toolbox begins to fill with new resources to try. Your hope grows as you see how God is at work in other settings.

As part of the Evangelistic Momentum efforts of the campus ministry of Campus Crusade for Christ, efforts are underway to create a learning culture focused on student evangelism. This learning environment is being fueled by lessons learned by local leaders engaged in front line ministry with today's students. This is why we are offering *The 250*, a publication to help stimulate your thinking on evangelism by gathering the best of what we have discovered so far from campus ministries across the country.

New initiatives and lessons learned are typically communicated vertically through reporting relationships or horizontally through the "grapevine" of personal connections. That, of course, is valuable to those who are exposed. But too often, laborers and leaders who would profit greatly from the ideas or initiatives of another team never have the opportunity to learn about them.

During April 2003, local leaders from more than 170 of our campus ministries across the U.S. were interviewed about their experiences in evangelism. These ministries represented Catalytic, Ethnic Student Ministries, Staffed Campuses and Bridges International. In a future edition, we plan to harvest ideas from our WSN partnerships and global campus partners. Wouldn't it be exciting to see ideas coming from Asia, Africa, India, Japan, Europe, and South America?

The results of these interviews were so exciting that we were compelled to share them with you. Why? There are at least five reasons to give you this edition of *The 250*.

1 >> To Spur Creativity

Ideas are the seedbed of creativity. When creative ideas begin to grow, they spawn innovation and innovation leads to progress.

The 250 is a treasury of ideas. But it is more than a top ten list. It is a compilation of more than 250 ideas. Yet they are not just ideas. Virtually every one has been tried on one or more campuses.

That, of course, doesn't mean that they are all equally effective. You can't simply look through the list, choose a couple and plop and play. Rather, the ideas in *The 250* are to stimulate your creativity. You can adapt what has been done at one campus to your situation.

Introduction continued...

Think of the three levels of innovation: improvement, evolution and invention.

The first level is improvement. Improvement occurs when you take something and make it better. Plenty of ideas in this book can improve your setting to make it more effective.

Evolution is the second level. Evolution occurs when you use one thing to make something new and different. It's not simply a better edition of the same idea. It's something new. But it grew out of that which preceded it. Many ideas here could evolve into something new, fresh and effective.

The third level of innovation is invention. Invention produces something altogether new. Invention occurs when people think about what could be, rather than what already is. You will find examples of invention in *The 250*. Hopefully, they will stimulate you to think "outside the box" and add your own new and creative strategies and methods to the Campus Crusade storehouse of evangelism resources.

2 ›› To Stimulate Learning

A primary means for any organization to expand its capacity (and thus its ability to accomplish its ultimate objectives) is through learning. The more we learn the more effective we become. Richard Karash wrote, "A 'Learning Organization' is one in which people at all levels, individually and collectively, are continually increasing their capacity to produce results they really care about."

What do we in the campus ministry deeply care about? Turning lost students into Christ-centered laborers. That process begins with effective evangelism. Evangelism is what we do best (or desire to do best). It's our passion and the engine that drives the rest of our ministry. In the words of Jim Collins, it's our Hedgehog Principle (From Good to Great, 2002).

Too often the good ideas, lessons learned or best practices in evangelism stay local. They are shared within the local team and that is good, for we desire to foster local learning teams. But we need to take the next step. We need to share the wealth across the organization so everyone learns and grows. We need to be a learning organization, especially in evangelism.

The 250 should serve as a catalyst in our learning culture.

3 ›› To Help You Plan Strategically

When it comes to strategic planning, evangelism is on everyone's plan. But often the tactics associated with it fail to measure up to our mission and vision.

But there is a better way to plan for evangelism. Rather than simply listing a number of tactics under the evangelism path step, effective teams are creating a strategic plan for evangelism itself. Path steps are organized around the modes of evangelism – ministry witness, natural witness and body witness. Prayer and training and development are added to them as additional path steps, providing a solid framework to begin adding tactical plans.

The 250 is designed to assist you in strategic planning for evangelism. Evangelism examples are organized around the five critical path steps— the three modes, prayer, and training and development. So if you're brainstorming ideas for natural evangelism, you can turn to the appropriate section and read what other campuses have tried.

4 ›› To Evaluate Your Effectiveness

Evaluation is a key to progress. It does not threaten our work though it may sometimes feel that way. It is essential to our work. It's the means by which we know we are effective.

One of the benefits of looking at what others have done is that it leads us to evaluate what we have been doing. In some cases, you will discover new insights that will help your strategies become more effective. In other cases, you may be able to share insights that will help others.

Be careful. Don't fall prey to the comparison trap. Rather, use evaluation to improve effectiveness, to grow and to develop. The end result should not be guilt. Rather, the honest look should provide insights into steps you can take to move forward, areas to build up, and how you can take advantage of new opportunities.

5 ›› To Celebrate Victories

While *The 250* is a compilation of evangelism initiatives and ideas, it is also a testimony to what God is doing in and through the efforts of all involved in Campus Crusade's outreach on the U.S. universities and colleges. Only eternity will reveal all the lives that have been touched by the strategies and methods contained in this edition. But as you read through this with the eyes of faith, may your heart rejoice over all the ways God has been at work.

The 250 reflects the apostle Paul's words from 1 Corinthians 9:19,22:

..To win as many as possible..by all possible means!

Keith Davy
Director of Research and Development

Five years of
IDEAS
from around the world

Need outreach or evangelism ideas?
Then you need to visit...

www.CampusStories.org

www.CampusStories.org is a large collection of student ministry strategies and stories that Campus Crusade staff from around the world have sent in over the last five years.

Browse through categories such as Audience, Launching/Critical Mass, Evangelism, and Discipleship/Sending or search by Date or Region.

Hundreds of good strategy ideas and motivating stories are waiting.

Prayer Evangelism

Evangelism is first and foremost a work of God. Therefore, the place to begin your evangelism is always with prayer. Prayer aligns us with the work of God and allows us the privilege of participating in his unfolding plan.

Certainly we need to pray for evangelism and the spread of the gospel. For example, Paul often exhorted the believers to pray for his witness to others (Colossians 4: 3,4), even as he prayed for the salvation of his own people (Romans 10:1). Later, you will read examples of campuses praying for evangelism.

But there are fresh winds blowing in the spiritual atmosphere of our culture. With these breezes has come openness to prayer as a common spiritual experience. The majority of people today claim prayer as part of their regular way of life. Though there is great divergence in whom they pray to and how they pray, the act of prayer can be common ground. In light of these realities, many have discovered prayer to be an effective means of outreach-praying not only for evangelism, but also prayer as evangelism.

Southern Connecticut
State University

PRAYER PRECEDES REVIVAL ON FOOTBALL TEAM

by Christian Martin

> "Sowing in prayer reaped the blessing God had for our ministry."

Praying in front of the school library every day at 7:30a.m, for several months, may seem like a hard pill to swallow, but for the ministry at Southern Connecticut State University, it was the way God brought them together to see more than 20 football players receive Christ!

"One of the guys in our ministry is on the football team," staff member Christian Martin said, "and one day the coach approached him to ask if he knew any pastors that would like to be a chaplain for the football team." Christian said Pastor Rick started a Bible study with the players on Friday afternoons, and after a few months, more than 20 football players accepted Christ into their hearts -- even the head coach gave his life to the Lord!

"When He said we reap what we sow, He meant it," Christian said. "Sowing in prayer reaped the blessing God had for our ministry." ✱

2》 How Can We Pray for You?
One of the Bible studies at North Carolina State went door-to-door in the dorms and asked students one simple question: "How can we pray for you?" They used a prayer sheet to help remember all the requests. The next week, the group followed-up with those who asked for prayer with questions like "How's your mother doing?" and "How did you do on that test?" The group was amazed by how open people were to prayer.

3》 Faithful to 5
Oklahoma State is using the Lighthouse Strategy (Prayer, Care, and Share) to reach the campus. Students were challenged to come up with five names of friends they know that they can pray for, care for, and share with. For some, it's the first time to share with someone they know personally. One girl kept praying for her friend during the year. Then one day, they went out to eat together. The girl asked if

MORE PRAYER EVANGELISM IDEAS 》

she could pray before she ate. Praying before a meal was a big step of faith for her.

4)) Prayer Table a Spin on the Publicity Table

The students at LSU set up a table right in front of the student union, asking students for prayer requests. On the prayer cards, students could write their first name, prayer requests, and whether they wanted someone to contact them. Many students revealed significant things on those prayer cards. Campus Crusade did not post their banner above the table; they wanted to pray for their peers, not promote the campus movement.

5)) Prayer Circle

Every Thursday at noon, Morgan State students meet in a circle to pray at areas of campus that experience high foot traffic. This public prayer circle is especially common and accepted in the African-American community. Other Christian groups are encouraged to join.

6)) Science and Prayer: Do They Mix?

At John Hopkins Nursing School, Campus Crusade created a partnership with Nurses Christian Fellowship and organized a prayer table. The theme was "We'd like to pray for you." In one hour, prayer requests ranged from concerns regarding the war and the economy, to more personal requests about children and classes. Snacks were also provided.

Ministry Evangelism

Through the years, Campus Crusade has been known for our intentional and strategic efforts in ministry evangelism. We have had the privilege of sharing Christ with countless college students who otherwise might not have had the opportunity to consider Christ. Evangelism in the ministry mode occurs when we intentionally reach out to another person with the purpose of witnessing to them (in contrast to the natural mode, in which we share with someone because of our relationship or natural connection). But ministry evangelism doesn't all look the same. There are countless examples of creative approaches, both to engage an audience and to communicate relevantly to them. The examples that follow will give you a taste of the creativity being used across campuses today.

LA Metro Team

CELL PHONE EVANGELISM

BY JODY HANFORD

" Call your Grandmother. "

Imagine cell phone themed posters all

around your campus that say, "If the person on the other end was God, would you take the call?"

That's how students at Mt. San Antonio College tapped into the electronic culture with a cell phone outreach, thanks to one student's unlimited calling plan.

After two weeks of advertising, Campus Crusade students set up a table with a pop-up tent and blown-up versions of the flyers hanging off the side. Signs were also posted saying, "Free Cell Phone Calls Anywhere in the US" and "Call your Grandmother."

Before making their call, students who came to the table were asked to go through a customized survey that included the question, "If God called in on your cell phone, what is one question you would like to ask Him?" Students and staff shared the "Knowing God Person-

ally" booklet and three students trusted Christ during the outreach! ✱

8 ⟩⟩ Target Areas Revisited

In our niche society, the University of Northern Colorado avoids campus-wide evangelism events. Instead, they focus on community groups, like students in the theatre program. Bible studies each have a vision/outreach leader, and each of the groups owns a target area. These leaders chart the course for developing relationships with the students in their specific target area and organize outreaches throughout the semester. Rather than bringing in major speakers, the ministry pours energy and attention into the small groups, helping the students learn the art of sowing seeds with those they see every day.

9 ⟩⟩ Broken Art Show

Students at the Maryland Institute and College of Art in Baltimore held an art show under the theme of "Broken." The students reserved the gallery and arranged all the art. The show lasted several weeks and hundreds of people

MORE MINISTRY EVANGELISM IDEAS ⟩⟩

came through to visit. The guest book signatures record a mix of faculty, staff members and students.

10 »> "Are You Ashamed?" Campaign

At New York University, the ministry organized an outreach called "Are You Ashamed?" They promoted the event with T-shirts, and one speaker used a historical survey of Christianity to address issues like the Holocaust and the Crusades.

11 »> Business Student Outreach

To reach his peers in the business department at the University of Texas, one student invited a business professional each week to discuss how his or her Christian faith played a significant role in the workplace. Named after the business term "return on investment," ROI met in the business school.

12 »> EveryStudent.com on Card Stock

Students at Northern Arizona University wanted to motivate more students to visit EveryStudent.com. So they created prominent card stock signs and posted them on stakes around campus in strategic locations. One series of signs, placed near the engineering school, provided a variety of reasons to believe in God. Another series of signs, placed in a heavily traveled walkway between the student union and the bookstore, listed six or seven reasons to save sex for marriage. All of the content came from EveryStudent.com articles and the Web site was printed at the bottom of each sign. Printed using a simple, readable font, the signs drew attention - every night more than 25% of them would be knocked down.

13 »> Stop the Presses! With Real Life News

A yearly newspaper is published by the UC Davis ministry. Each year Real Life News focuses the content around a special speaker, such as Darrell Scott. The first year it included ESC ads and articles from Rusty Wright and Dick Purnell. They print 5,000 copies of the 12-page paper for only 10 cents a copy and hand it out at lecture halls and around campus.

14 »> "Hey, I did a 180!"

The Twin Cities Metro ministry expanded an idea born at UW River Falls three years earlier. On the metro web site, students posted their photographs with their testimonies. Next, the picture/testimony combos were printed out in poster form and table tents to distribute on the individual campuses. "Hey, I did a 180!" became the theme of the outreach and several campuses within the metro area hosted a special speaker and invited students to publicly describe their testimony. Since many students prepared their personal testimonies, the "180 Campaign" provided long-term success as well.

15 »> If We Are Only Matter, Do We Matter?

The ministry think-tank at Yale University prepared a campaign called "Think About It." Ads, posters and discussion groups posed the question, "If we are only matter, do we matter?" Discussion groups with humanists and Buddhists on campus followed.

16 »> Soul Inside?

They wanted to stimulate spiritual conversations on the campus of Dartmouth College. The group created a campaign, complete with a logo-a yellow caution sign with a person looking down at a hole in their heart, and the cryptic question: Soul Inside? Some posters featured prominent people like Mother Teresa and Princess Diana, and asked: Where are they after their death? The campaign included ads and articles in the school paper, dorm discussions and lectures. They hosted a multi-faith panel discussion, and gave away Bibles and other books.

17 >> "What Bugs You About Religion?"

At the University of New Mexico, the ministry runs five to six ESC campaigns per year, seeing a few students respond via e-mail for more information each time. The students created their own campaign titled: "What bugs you about religion?" To kick it off they had students submit quotes of what they didn't like about religion and then had a grad student write an article in response. More than 60 e-mails came in as a result with some as long as three pages. Each one was telling things that bothered people about religion. The ministry followed up via e-mail and met with willing students.

18 >> "I'm all ears" Campaign

You can speak volumes if you just listen. At the University of Florida, staff members and students promised a listening ear, inviting students to meet them at a certain place to offer their point of view. They utilized the student newspaper, emphasizing that anyone who came would be listened to closely. The campaign included T-shirts promising, "I'm all ears."

19 >> "Who do you think I am?" Campaign

Based on Jesus' question in Luke 9:20, the UC Santa Barbara ministry ran a campaign titled "Who do you think I am?" T-shirts, posters and the school newspaper were all utilized to draw attention to Jesus and famous quotes about Him. They also included quotes from professors at the school. The campaign concluded with a local pastor sharing who Jesus is as explained in the Bible.

20 >> "Real Life" Campaign Accomplishes Coverage

A multi-faceted campaign called "Real Life" at Ball State created a wide spectrum of opportunities for students to share, no matter where they were in their Christian maturity. At the core of the outreach, leaders of the movement placed Every Students Choice ads in the paper. Simultaneously, students and staff members wore "Real Life" T-shirts with EveryStudent.com publicized on them. The messages at the weekly meetings were also coordinated with the campaign. The "Real Life" campaign was very effective in terms of coverage. Students knew about it all over campus and there were many opportunities for personal evangelism. Bible study groups also paired up to share the gospel on campus.

21 >> What to Wear for Great Sex

One popular ESC campaign ad addresses the question of sex before marriage by stating, "What to wear for great sex" along with the picture of wedding rings. The ministry of Boise State ran this campaign during condom week on campus and as an enhancement passed out gold rings to further solidify the point with students.

22 >> Buses for Jesus

Penn State thought of a creative and cost effective way to get people thinking about God. The ministry rented ad space inside the local buses and prepared five separate ads about the attributes of God. Each ad ran on 50-60 buses with the potential to be seen more than 4 million times. Topics included God's goodness, mercy and justice, and included the ministry web site. The ads cost the equivalent of a page ad in the paper for one day. Next year they plan to run the ads again and will use them to highlight their weekly meeting.

23 >> Pass the Salt

Kent State wanted to spice up conversations on campus, so they made T-shirts with the words, "Pass the Salt." Everyone wore their shirts on the same day, generating questions about the meaning. In response, staff members and students spoke about God and invited people to the weekly meeting.

24 >> Are you Empty?

With the word "Empty" plastered on the back of T-shirts, students at Cal State Fresno engaged their peers in spiritual conversations. What do people do to fill the emptiness in their lives? As a part of the campaign, several students explained how they were rescued from a place of emptiness.

25 >> EveryStudent.com, Literally

Over a two-week period the ministry at Ohio University blitzed the campus with EveryStudent.com coverage. An email was sent to every student and letters were stuffed in student mailboxes. They utilized posters and newspaper ads as well.

26 >> "Code Red" Odor Warning

James Madison University's Campus Crusade has blazed trails with using the EveryStudent.com site. T-shirts were printed with the words "Code Red" and included the Web site address. Prizes were awarded to those students who wore their shirts the most consecutive days.

27 >> $50 Web Site Outreach

At UC Davis the ministry passed out several thousand cards inviting people to their site where they could register to win $50. On the site they found banners like, "If you were to die today, how sure are you that you would go to heaven?"

28 >> Movie Night Intermission

At Albuquerque Community College, the ministry invites the whole campus to come to a movie night. During the movie, they have an intermission: students fill out a questionnaire, which later is used to pull a name for a gift raffle and for spiritual follow-up later.

29 >> PurdueQuestions.org

Posters advertising the Web site PurdueQuestions.org covered the campus of Purdue for several weeks during the semester. Once students visit the site they have options to read a number of ESC articles.

Natural Evangelism

Throughout the day, our paths naturally intersect the lives of many individuals. These natural connections provide many opportunities to be a witness for Christ. For staff members, as outsiders in the campus community, natural opportunities are harder to come by. For students, as insiders, they abound. Often these connections come as divine appointments, when God orchestrates the circumstances to bring two people together. But in many ways we can be intentional at both fostering relationships and creating the environment in which significant conversations about the gospel occur.

Lighthouse

University of Arkansas

by Hunter Hall

> "We have asked students only to live in relational and body life and the only time we do ministry evangelism is for training purposes."

We continue to emphasize being intentional with relational evangelism. We have had two semesters worth of Lighthouse strategy training and we are seeing students come to faith sometimes as long as a year after someone initiated with them.

To make it practical, we take an aspect of the Lighthouse strategy over one semester. Each month is a mode where one part of the strategy is emphasized. For example, the first month is spent in prayer. Praying for people to pray for, praying for them specifically and praying for opportunities to relate and share with them. The second month is the month of caring. We spend time brainstorming ways to communicate care, how we can do random acts of kindness and we revisit how things are going every two weeks.

The third month we focus on opportunities to share with the people that we've been praying and caring for.

Most of the relationships take much longer than three months to build. We keep a poster board of names of all the students we're praying for as a visual reminder. We have asked students only to live in relational and body life and the only time we do ministry evangelism is for training purposes. Our desire is to position students for a relational approach to evangelism. *

31 >> Book on the Desk Corner Ministry
Curiosity may have killed a cat, but one New Jersey businessman figured curiosity might also help save someone. He bought a number of copies of the books "Darwin's Black Box" and "Mere Christianity." He then offered to give a copy to students at Princeton if the students would agree to place the book on the corner of their desks for one month and use it to initiate conversations. Around 50 students

accepted the challenge and were able to initiate conversations with those who sat close by.

32 >> Art Institute Sports Outreach

Creativity is no problem for students at the Art Institute of Chicago. To draw attention, surface interested people, and develop friendships, the students advertised a running club. They advertised the club with scenes from the movie Chariots of Fire, placing cutouts of their own heads atop the actor's bodies. Posters and flyers bear the tongue-in-cheek question, "Who says there's no sports here?"

33 >> Detroit Day of Faith

During the One Day of Faith nationwide campaign, the Detroit Metro team carried out the strategy citywide. For six weeks leading up to the event, they led the prayer, care and share strategy.

34 >> Sprint PCS - This is not a commercial

The Impact Movement at Tennessee State University tried to think of ways to be more involved in the lives of students. During the spring, they launched a campaign that they called Sprint PCS. These letters stand for Prayer, Care and Share. The campaign included 2 weeks of praying through a list of specific people (Prayer). Then there were 2 weeks of looking for ways to get involved in the lives of these same people (Care). Finally there were two weeks set aside for initiating opportunities to share Christ with these same people. The Impact students focused on carrying out the PCS campaign after each Bible study.

35 >> Prayer-Care-Share Cards

The ministry at Southern Methodist University printed prayer/care/share cards that unfold and guide students on this familiar technique for reaching their friends. They are encouraged to pray for five people, act on specific ways to care for these people and then share Christ with them. Entire Bible studies are challenged to get personally involved with other students in this way.

36 >> Dinner and an Invite

Want a creative way to get more students to your weekly meeting? The ministry at the University of Louisiana in Lafayette passed out 40 Chili's gift certificates ($10 each) to students. They were instructed to take a friend with them to dinner and invite their friend to join them at CRU.

37 >> Faith Flags

Cincinnati Metro encouraged their students to look for ways to plant "faith flags" in the midst of their everyday conversations. Students are able to identify themselves as Christians simply by saying something like, "I prayed before I took the test today." These simple statements allow students to communicate to their friends that there is a dimension to their lives that they had not previously known about.

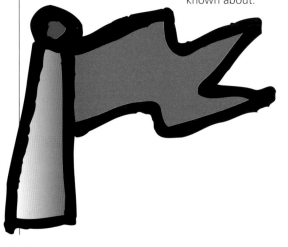

38» **Art Thou Saved?**

One block from the University of New Mexico, a church meets in a converted movie theatre. The lobby of the church is made available for students to display their artwork. A group of artistic students meets at the church to create art and to discuss the meaning of their art. This has opened up doors to talk about the gospel.

39» **Battle of the Bands**

Students at Drexel University in Philadelphia sponsored a battle of the bands on campus. Many of the students are musically talented and saw this as an opportunity to develop relationships with the people who came out to the concert. The event was not billed or perceived as a religious gathering.

40» **Weekly Meeting Welcome Gifts**

At the beginning of every Campus Crusade meeting at Rutgers University, all the new people are asked to raise their hands. Each new person receives a coupon to exchange for a gift at the meeting's end. As the students exit the meeting room, student leaders and staff members stand at the door and give a gift package that includes a response card. Because the gospel is shared each week, one question on the card is: Did you receive Christ tonight?

41» **Leadership Expectation: Join a Group**

Arkansas Metro student leaders are expected to get involved in another student group with freshmen involved. They are encouraged to join with a friend in order to build relationships with non-believers. The desired outcome is that the Campus Crusade leaders will have opportunities to share their faith within these relationships at some point during the year. This is also a great way to model relational ministry to other students in the movement.

42» **Ministry to Free Thinkers**

A couple of key students at Michigan State began attending the "Free Thinkers" club on campus. The common belief among members is atheism. The Christians go to build relationships and so far the group has been accepting of them. Michigan State students are strategically placed in different influential clubs on campus.

43» **Just Be Who You Are**

The San Francisco Metro team is challenging students to live out the principle of being set apart, but not separate from the culture around them. They want to see their students involved in other clubs on campus - art club, dance team, or intramural sports. In this way, students are learning that in ministry you don't have to create your own thing, but you can just be who you are.

44» **4-Wheeling for Christ**

Students involved in the Michigan Tech ministry joined clubs on campus to build relationships with non-Christians. One of the most popular activities in the area is 4-wheeling, so some of the students signed up for this unique field of ministry.

45 >> Connecting with Campus Leaders

At UNC Chapel Hill, a leadership organization holds a summit once a week for presidents of campus clubs. The student president of Campus Crusade attends.

46 >> Intramural Sports All the Way

At North Carolina State, 100 students participate in intramural softball. The students are encouraged to join other teams and build relationships that can lead to evangelistic opportunities.

47 >> Combining Ministry with Interests

Arizona State's Campus Crusade has encouraged students to form their ministry around affinity groups. Examples include a freshman group of guys who like to play racquetball who can form their evangelism around reaching other guys in the racquetball club. This is helping students to have an intentional focus with their evangelism.

48 >> Coffeehouse Success

The ministry at the University of Central Florida hosts a successful coffeehouse where students can see a community of Christians in a normal environment. The ministry also opens the coffeehouse for other clubs on campus to use. The coffeehouse helps integrate new people who show up at their weekly meetings because of the relational and comfortable environment. People from extremely diverse backgrounds hang out at the coffeehouse and interact with the Christian students there.

49 >> Living on Campus with Purpose

While most upper classmen choose off-campus housing, Campus Crusade students at Iowa State choose to live on campus in order to build relationships with students. The upperclassmen trade in their privacy for cafeteria food, midnight fire drills and community showers so that they can meet and mentor a freshman or sophomore.

50 >> Committed to the Dorms

At the Minnesota State University - Moorhead, 14 guys are moving back into a dorm to focus on reaching that dorm. They organized a regular game of "capture the flag" and other activities to foster relationships with their dorm mates.

Body Evangelism

Whenever the body of Christ is gathered, it has the potential of being used by God as a powerful witness. A healthy body of believers is filled with love and truth, the very thing people desire to experience. The environment of love and truth not only provides an environment for believers to grow, it also provides an ideal setting for individuals to come to Christ. This may occur in large groups and small. It may occur in planned meetings or informal social gatherings. Ministries across the nation are discovering how to open the doors of their community to allow outsiders to enter and experience the love and truth of Christ flowing through the witness of the body.

Saddleback College

EXTREME DAYS

BY DAVE THORNSBERRY

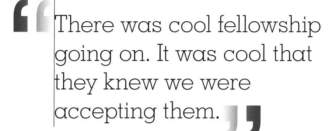

" There was cool fellowship going on. It was cool that they knew we were accepting them. "

At Saddleback College, Campus Crusade is seen in the eyes of non-believers as being more of a club rather than a ministry. However, students this year accelerated their evangelism efforts through club-to-club contacts.

In December, with final exams only half a week away, Campus Crusade students scheduled a party/outreach.

The strategy was to have an all-campus showing of the movie EXTREME DAYS on a Wednesday evening in the middle of campus. A number of students from the Poetry Club, including its president, attended the Campus Crusade event. The Poetry Club is known as a very secular and morally liberal group, with many of its members also involved with the Pagan Club.

Sarah Moor, Campus Crusade student leader, shares, "There was cool fellowship going on. It was cool that they knew we were accepting them."

EXTREME DAYS was a hit with almost everyone present. After the showing, the Poetry Club members invited the Campus Crusade students to their 9PM poetry reading.

Campus Crusade student leader, Mike Morabito, attended the reading and comments, "Their poetry had a lot to do with their spiritual hunger and search."

Sarah Moor brimmed with excitement as she described the more over-arching effects of the evangelistic movie outreach. "We had felt this weird kind of oppression on campus towards us from some of the Poetry Club and Pagan Club members. We had heard that they liked us as individuals, but that as a group there is something about Campus Crusade that oppresses them." Moor continues, "They seemed surprised that we wanted to hang out with them." *

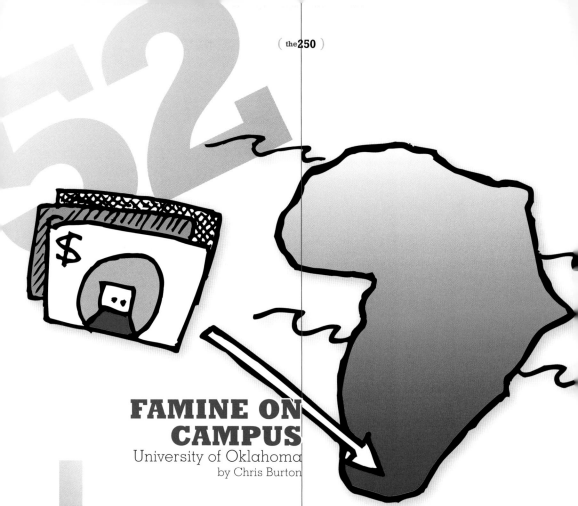

FAMINE ON CAMPUS
University of Oklahoma
by Chris Burton

Last fall, 20/20 featured a story about the famine in South Africa-reported to be the worst humanitarian problem in the world and the most severe in the last decade. That led the ministry at the University of Oklahoma to form a campus-wide campaign called the Sower Project that not only helped raise money for South Africa but also put student leaders in contact with more than 60 different campus organizations, including Greek houses, academic fraternities, and ethnic student groups.

The project, which the university supported, asked students to participate in a two-day famine. During that time students who gave up a meal, or a day

> **During that time students who gave up a meal, or a day of meals, gave the money they would have spent to an organization that helps South Africa.**

of meals, gave the money they would have spent to an organization that helps South Africa.

Most of the campus organizations participated and students donated about $19,000 to help South Africa-- a figure the government will match. Plus, the ministry's student leaders met and spent time with people from most of the university clubs. ✱

53 ›› Party with a Purpose at Ball State

Ball State is not known as a big party school, but that doesn't stop the Campus Crusade movement from using parties as a cool way to connect with the lost. The staff and student leaders say they want the Campus Crusade parties to be the kind of thing that students are still talking about on Monday mornings. Their parties are all the fun, minus the alcohol, of typical college parties. On one occasion, with 150 students packed into a party at one house, the cops stopped by suspicious of finding trouble. Needless to say, the authorities were pleasantly surprised.

54 ›› Michigan State's Dorm Focused Weekly Meeting

One week the team at Michigan State moved their weekly meeting in front of a dorm housing 300 students. The whole event was geared toward serving and reaching the residents of that dorm. Customized surveys spoke specifically to the needs of students there. Several servant evangelism activities were included in the evening. A buzz was created and the students realized that their peers from Campus Crusade really cared about them.

55 ›› You Bring the Popcorn, We've Got the Movie

The Jesus Film? Not this time. Southern Oregon University students found "movie hang-out time" to be effective in developing relationships with non-Christians. Every week, Campus Crusade students invite several non-Christian friends to watch a movie. No spiritual content is included, but doors are opened to getting into each others' lives more down the road.

56 ›› What Would Jesus Do About the Poor?

Portland Metro approached a partnership with Amnesty International and the Jewish Student group at Reed College to host a "Poverty Awareness Week." During the course of the week, they brought in speakers and raised awareness about the needs of the poor. The entire student body was challenged to try living on just $3 a day. This provided opportunities for Christians to share about Jesus' view of the poor and how He treated them.

57 ›› Soup Kitchen serves up relationships with non-Christians

Reed College has a lot of student groups focused on humanitarian concerns. Seizing this reality, the Campus Crusade students organize a weekly trip down to a soup kitchen. Many who agree to come are non-Christians. While providing practical help to the needy off the streets, the Christians are interacting with unbelievers from their campus. They see Christians providing real love to people who are very different from who they see on campus all the time. One participant with Campus Crusade asks non-Christians about why they came to help. This usually leads to the question being reciprocated and an opportunity to talk being a follower of Jesus and how Jesus cares for the poor.

58 ›› Get Wet: University of Montana Take Freshmen Rafting

Freshmen expect adventure in college. Campus Crusade at the University of Montana aims to deliver just that. The ministry handed out Freshmen Survival Kits for two days when the freshmen first arrived. Along with the kit, they handed out a sheet listing all the fall events, including a water excursion. On Labor Day, they hosted the rafting trip. The experience was innexpensive for the students who came, and there was a BBQ party after the rafts left the water. About 50 students showed up last year.

59 >> **Connecting With Diverse Groups**

Baltimore Metro has looked for ways to build bridges to other groups on campus. They have found that doing service projects together is a helpful way to form relationships. On one of their campuses they teamed up with a homosexual group to do a food drive. Through the activity, the students got a chance to know the Christians and some even attended a Bible study. The two groups got to know each other in a non-threatening environment. Some of the students from the other group had been raised in church and were interested in checking out what Campus Crusade was about.

60 >> **Weekly Meeting Seeking the Seeker**

Marshal University has positioned its weekly meeting to attract those seeking more understanding about God. The talk is geared toward both Christians and non-Christians. Each week there are fun give-a-ways and the meeting wraps up with lots of music at the end.

61 >> **Attention Getting Topics Fuel Weekly Meeting**

Staff and students at the University of North Carolina are finding ways to touch the culture of their campus. Each week the meeting focuses on a topic and unpacks how that issue is addressed from a Christian perspective verses what society offers.

62 >> **Socials Get a Thumbs Up in Tampa**

Strategy for evangelism in Tampa centers around bringing non-Christians into the activities of Christian friends. Once a month the ministry carries out a relational outreach. One month they did a camping trip with several non-Christians attending. For Easter they hosted a pizza dinner. Other ideas include renting out a gym and hanging out at a coffee shop. The legwork before hand is to align the Christian students to the idea that these are meant to be more than just social gatherings.

63 >> **Tuesday Night Community-Groups at Auburn**

The ministry at Auburn has seen good relational ministry taking place in community groups. Structured like a cell group, the men's and women's groups meet on Tuesday nights for about 20 minutes of teaching and then they break up into smaller groups for discussion. They are building an evangelism component into the community groups and next fall they will begin a freshman co-ed community group.

64 >> **Spreading Out Leadership in Community Groups**

The University of Alabama is adjusting their community group strategy to include more students in a leadership role. Each of their groups have four students serving in four different roles depending on their skills and gifts. The idea seems to be working as the groups are growing in number and size. The Christians enjoy the relational setting and can invite their friends. Non-Christians are invited into the community groups before becoming a Christian. Each group is discussion oriented and Alabama has found that students will most likely come to a community group before coming to an evangelistic outreach.

Training and Development

One major reason we don't share our faith is that we are not quite sure what to say or do. Training becomes a key in overcoming this obstacle. Training and development can take on many forms, but the outcomes are clear. Being equipped in evangelism not only inspires confidence, it increases effectiveness. Effective training and development increases the number of laborers in the harvest, essential for a ministry devoted to reaching students for Christ.

65》 Evangelism Model Training

At Ball State, Campus Crusade leaders offered an evangelism planning time to prepare for the upcoming school year. Staff members explained the three modes of evangelism, and then, in the room, they created a station representing each mode. They invited students to brainstorm different ideas and write them down at each station. Every idea was written down and compiled for the new evangelism team to consider next year.

66》 Bringing in the Local Community

Campus Crusade's Development Council at Stanford met together and brainstormed new evangelism ideas. They invited a local businessman to facilitate the idea-driven session.

67》 Contagious Christian

University of Oregon is using Bill Hybel's curriculum and book, "Becoming a Contagious Christian" to motivate their students to a lifestyle of evangelism. Evangelism, the curriculum explains, is more than random surveys; students learn that their natural niche can be the best place to share their faith.

68》 Three Fridays

At Washington State University, Campus Crusade students offer an evangelism-training workshop called "Three Fridays." The entire workshop is student-led. They give a Biblical basis for initiative evangelism and then discuss how to go from chitchat to the gospel. In addition, they play a tape from Campus Crusade's 1999 U.S. Staff Conference, featuring radio host and author Ron Hutchcraft on how to bring an unchanging message to a changing culture.

69》 Money Talks

During spring break, Campus Crusade students in the Baltimore area go on a weekend retreat together each year. It's a low-key version of "Big Break" in Panama City. Each team gets $20 to use the money for a creative way to reach out to someone. Teams will clean someone's house and leave a Bible or share a testimony. The hope is that by the end of the day, students will have found many different ways to share the gospel.

70》 Survey Says

At Howard University, staff members use the beginning of the semester to train their students on how to conduct a questionnaire. The training covers four subjects: behavior, values, belief, and worldview. In addition, the students develop their own spiritual surveys; they must choose a passage of scripture that relates back to their topic of choice. The training actually happens, though, when the students go out and share their faith and then debrief afterwards.

71》 Evangelism Explosion

The IMPACT team at the University of Virginia hosted an evangelism training time for students on a Sunday afternoon. About 20 students attended and were equipped for the day of evangelism explosion when students went into the dining halls and conducted surveys with every African American. They also distributed copies of the IMPACT CD.

72》 The Journey

Staff members with the Washington DC Metro Team began training their students through the "CoJourners" guide developed by Keith Davy. The booklet helps the student identify four primary roles that they can play in another person's spiritual journey. The "Co-Journer" guide has changed students' views on sharing their faith. The students used to see evangelism as an event, but this guide has helped students see evangelism as a process, something positive and that's easy to do.

73 >> The Gospel in the Marketplace

At the University of Alabama, Campus Crusade staff members offer an opportunity in the spring for students to hear about evangelism in the marketplace. They invite recent graduates back to speak to the students about what it's like to share their faith at work.

74 >> Mini Big Break

An evangelistic opportunity for Campus Crusade students at Arizona State University is organizing their own spring break outreach. A huge attraction for college students, the event is held at Rocky Point, the closest beach to Arizona on the sea of Cortez.

75 >> Berkeley Blitz

At Berkeley, students watched a black and white video of a Berkeley Blitz back in the 60's. One student wanted a blitz for this generation. As a result, 35 people volunteered to help with the outreach team. The group was commissioned specifically for a weeklong outreach.

Looking Back

Students on the
evangelism team
at James Madison
University are
committed to seeing
their campus reached for
Christ. So committed, in fact, that they
are willing to take an extra step after an
outreach…Evaluation.

> "Evaluation helps us assess the effectiveness of the outreach and this is glorifying to God."

"Evaluation is the missing link of strategic planning. It's supposed to be part of the process. But most leaders are too busy moving ahead to take the time to look back. As a result, they miss the very insights that would help them move forward more effectively," says Keith Davy.

Take a look as JMU looks back on a recent outreach:

BACKGROUND: The number '420' is code or slang for marijuana, so April 20th is a pot-smoking holiday. This year, Easter fell on the same date. One student noticed the coincidence and had the idea of making t-shirts to encourage the campus to worship Christ rather than smoke up this Easter.

PROS: The gospel was shared more than 87 times in one week; people had over 602 conversations about Christ and got to tell their entire classes about Christ when professors asked about the t-shirts. Christians; had to step out of their comfort zone; to decide to wear the t-shirt [every day].

CONS: The outreach proved to be offensive to some Christians who were not involved with Crusade and who did not understand the outreach. Some people just didn't get the message that we were not promoting smoking pot.

SOLUTIONS: We should clarify how proactive people have to be in sharing their faith and telling people about the shirts rather then waiting for them to ask. Flyers also would have been helpful to hand to people as they were walking by if we didn't have a chance to tell them about the shirt.

Matt D'Antuono, a junior at JMU finds that, "Evaluation helps us assess the effectiveness of the outreach and this is glorifying to God. It is also important for future outreaches because the evangelism team is handed over to new leadership every year. It's useful for the new leaders to find out what worked and what didn't and we include suggestions about future outreaches so they're not starting from scratch." *

PACK FOR THE JOURNEY

Everyone is on a spiritual journey. But how do you enter
someone else's journey, helping them come to Jesus?

EXPLORER - discover where they are

GUIDE - show them the way to Jesus Christ

BUILDER - bridge the obstacles along the way

MENTOR - encourage them to press on

The journey to know God is uniquely individual and takes many turns. God desires to use us to help others find their way. What are practical steps students can take to intentionally enter a friend's journey? ¶ The CoJourners Pack is a resource providing small group leaders with 20 discussion cards to guide students toward an intentional lifestyle of evangelism. Include a card in your small group as a training nugget to help students take another step in evangelism. The 8-12 minute discussions highlight motivation for evangelism and the four roles listed above. ¶ To order your CoJourners Pack, contact New Life Resources: **800-827-2788** or visit: www.campuscrusade.org. Brought to you by your friends at Research & Development.

STUDENT GROUPS

ATHLETES »

76 » Pizza Party Evangelism

At the University of Virginia, evangelism looks like a pizza-eating contest. Each sports team from the athletic department picks a representative to compete, preferably the biggest eater. The teams join the fun by cheering on their favorite athlete. A local radio station comes out and free pizza is given away. At the end of the contest, one of the coaches explains how Christ changed his life.

77 » Inside Connection

East Tennessee State University suggests trying to become an insider with the athletic teams in order to build relationships. A Campus Crusade staff member serves as the chaplain for the football and basketball teams there. He travels with the teams and conducts a weekly team meeting. He also meets one-on-one with the guys and leads a discipleship group. Two of the football players he led to Christ have returned to the campus as coaches.

78 » Seeking Professional Help

At Louisiana State, a Campus Crusade staff member is the chaplain for the baseball team. Over the years, he has built a trusting relationship with the coach. Students who became professional baseball players have come back to speak and sometimes to even join the chaplain on some personal appointments.

79 » Super Bowl Outreach

The Jacksonville Metro team hosted a Super Bowl outreach in the lobby of a dorm. During halftime, two players from the Jacksonville Jaguars spoke to the group about how Jesus changed their lives.

80 » Campus Partnerships

South Dakota has the right idea about athletic partnerships. Both the University of South Dakota and South Dakota State created a partnership with Fellowship of Christian Athletes to bring in professional football players. South Dakota State invited former NFL player, Steven Grant, and the University of South Dakota invited a player with the Denver Broncos.

81 » Surf Evangelism

The San Diego Metro team hosted a viewing of the "Outsiders" which features professional surfer, Brian Jennings. A world champion and a recent believer, Brian shares his testimony on the video.

ETHNIC STUDENTS »

82 » Love Thy Neighbor

At the University of Texas, El Paso, the Destino Movement applied Christ's command to "Love thy neighbor." Another student organization had an office right next to Destino. The group, called Mecha, focused on political issues important to Americans of Mexican decent. The two groups organized a tailgate party together and are planning further shared parties and events. A few students from Mecha have come to Christ as a result of the relationships that are forming.

83 » IMPACT Forum

The Charleston Metro team has recently launched an IMPACT movement on one of their campuses. During African American month, they hosted a forum featuring a Christian minister or businessman who spoke on culturally relevant issues.

84 ›› Jesus Jam

At Morgan State in Baltimore, an African-American Bible study started something called Jesus Jam. A DJ plays Christian music and there is break-dancing and step-dancing. A Christian shares how Jesus changed his life and others are invited to publicly respond, giving their lives to Christ as well.

85 ›› A Step in the Right Direction

At Morgan State in Baltimore, the Alpha Omega group has ten chapters around the city. This African American organization is an alternative to a fraternity or sorority and they travel around performing step demonstrations. The school asked them to perform for potential freshman and it turned out to be a very effective outreach. The group will share a testimony and scripture.

86 ›› Team Work

The IMPACT movement at George Mason hosted a coffeehouse this year. They invited IMPACT students from another campus who had special talent. Campuses over an hour away came to help. There was scheduled talent, an open mic time, and evangelistic poetry and rap. It was very helpful to draw upon the resources of other IMPACT campuses.

87 ›› 3-on-3

At Mississippi State, Campus Crusade created a 3-on-3 basketball tournament to reach African Americans. Every applicant received a package containing the Olympics-themed version of the "Fallen But Not Forgotten" mini-mags, a T-shirt, a soda, candy, and a copy of Josh McDowell's evangelistic paperback, "More Than a Carpenter."

88 ›› Hip Hop Evangelism

At Syracuse University, Campus Crusade hosted the HipHopalypse, intended to attract African American rappers. Christian rap acts from New York City performed at the event. One of the rappers shared his testimony and the gospel.

89 ›› Women of Wisdom

At the University of Louisiana, Lafayette, one of the female staff members started visiting the African American sororities. She gave a talk on how to have a balanced life and from that was able to begin a focus group. During the focus group, the staff member began going through "The Passage," (a version of the Four Spiritual Laws designed with African Americans in mind), discussing one law a week. The group was investigative as they dug deeper into the gospel each week.

90 ›› Finding Their Identity

The Epic movement at UCLA hosted a seminar focusing on Asian Greeks. They brought in four prominent Asian Greeks who spoke on the Asian American identity. They also brought in an Asian American psychologist who shared his story. The seminar was set up as a pledge event; and so, many students attended for points.

91 >> Free Boba

The Epic movement at UCLA found a great way to publicize their weekly meeting. During orientation in the student union, Campus Crusade advertised that there would be free Boba at their weekly meeting. Boba is tapioca milk tea and very popular among Asians. Over 100 students attended the weekly meeting.

FRESHMEN>>

92 >> Get Wet

Freshmen crave adventure in college. At the University of Montana, Campus Crusade staff members played to that craving by sponsoring a Labor Day rafting trip. The day trip was included on a list of all the events planned for the fall by Campus Crusade, which freshmen received along with a Freshman Survival Kit during the first two days of school.

93 >> Break Up

Why use the FSK all at the same time when you can distribute the components separately to different audiences? That's a creative idea being used at Indiana University. After hosting a three-on-three basketball tournament, the losers all received a FSK as a consolation prize. In one of the fraternity houses, a student passed out 80 copies of the apologetic book, "A Case for Christ," and the Bibles were given to the football team.

94 >> Personalizing Evangelism

University of Wisconsin, LaCross doesn't distribute FSKs right at the beginning of the year. However, six weeks into the semester at Campus Crusade's fall retreat, students sign-up to give FSKs to their friends. This personalizes the evangelism and gives the freshman an opportunity to step out in faith.

95 >> The Cabinet

When it comes to FSKs, Baltimore Metro likes to spice things up a bit with coupons from local businesses and restaurants. After distribution, if there are extra pieces left over like the CDs, toys, or books, they add them to "The Cabinet." The Cabinet contains extra stock of the FSK items and students are free to take anything inside, as long as they give it to someone who doesn't know Christ.

96 >> Cup Advertising

George Mason University uses surveys with the FSKs. This year, they also added a white, plastic cup printed with their logo, meeting time and place.

97 ›› Going Hungry for Jesus

At East Tennessee State University, staff members include an evangelistic, freshman CD-ROM in the FSKs. The plan is to do it four years in a row. The project is student-funded and the students are challenged to give up one meal, reinvesting that money toward the project.

98 ›› Senior Days

The University of Southern Mississippi starts early with incoming freshmen. They pass out FSKs to every high-school senior attending high-school senior orientation days on campus. They also get their e-mail addresses in order to contact them in the fall.

99 ›› Strategic Location

Staff members at South Dakota State try to maximize campus events. Each fall, they set up a big banner between the main freshman dorm and the site of the "beginning-of-the-year picnic." From this prime location, they give away FSKs and root beer floats.

100 ›› An X-Box Giveaway

The University of South Dakota adds a bit of a twist to their FSK distribution by using an X-Box. Last year, when they distributed FSKs without the X-Box, they received a total of 196 surveys that included a variety of ages. This year when they used the X-Box, they collected 450 surveys that were only freshmen.

101 ›› Putting FSKs in the Right Hands

At Cal State, Chico, staff members make sure to get the FSKs in the hands of the influential people on campus. The RAs receive them so they will know what their dorm residents are receiving. Student leaders receive them, as well as Panhellenic counsel. The rest are distributed in front of the dining hall.

102 ›› Freshmen Dessert

The University of North Dakota hosted a dessert for their freshmen leaders. During this time, the ministry's vision is communicated in the hopes that they will learn the importance of reaching their freshmen class.

103 ›› Getting Plugged In

During the first week of school at the University of Florida, Campus Crusade rents out a rock climbing gym and lets the students use it for free for four hours. A band plays, appetizers are served, and the freshmen learn about the ministry.

104 ›› Direct Line

At Southwest Texas State, Campus Crusade came up with "Direct Line" strategy. A local telemarketing firm trained students in how to ask the right questions. The ministry bought the student database from the university and sent out postcards in advance to let people know that they would be contacted. The survey included questions like, "What made you come to Southwest?" and "What's been the hardest part of school?" Then the survey took a spiritual turn and asked, "Do you go to church?" and "Have you heard about Campus Crusade for Christ?" At the end, the student is offered either a FSK or a student planner. The students were paid to make the phone calls and at the end, they would rate how they felt the conversation went and whether or not the person was interested in getting involved. The calls generated thorough contacts for follow-up.

Baylor University
FIRST DAY OF CLASS

BY LORI FLEENER

> "On the night of the big social, pumping music and flying t-shirts filled the air."

Who doesn't like ice cream? Every Fall semester, Baylor students involved in CRU, Destino, and Impact throw an all-freshman Ice Cream Bash. Students organizing the annual event blitz the campus with advertising by stuffing 5,000 mailboxes, chalking the sidewalk, hanging up posters, and handing out flyers.

On the night of the big social, pumping music and flying t-shirts filled the air. Freshman Survival Kits were on hand, a Sony Playstation II was given away, and, of course there was ice cream. Nearly 500 students packed the room plus hundreds signed up for more information. Every name will be contacted for evangelism and discipleship.

"We are excited about reaching students of all ethnicities on campus," says staff member Lori Fleener, "and this event was a helpful and fruitful first step." *

106›› Ministry Brochure
Campus Crusade at Southwest Texas State designed a ministry brochure, and through a mailing company, they sent 5,000 copies to students' home addresses two weeks before school began.

107›› Camp Out
A camping trip is a great way to gather freshmen believers at Oklahoma State. To build momentum in the fall, the freshmen go on an overnight camping trip the first week of classes. The site is close to campus and the time serves to build relationships and to form a team of people to assist the ministry.

MORE FRESHMEN EVANGELISM IDEAS ››

108 >> Best of Boulder

The University of Boulder wanted to move to the next level with technology so they have been using the "Freshman Experience" CD. There are eight different interviews on the CD, including Christian and non-Christian points of view. The CD also includes information about Campus Crusade's weekly meetings and local churches. The CD is sent out to 6,000 on-campus freshmen and is set to arrive within the first couple days of school. A Nalgene bottle is given away to the first 100 students who fill out a survey through the CD. The cost is about $12,000.

109 >> Orientation With a Purpose

In the Chicago Metro area, upperclassmen come back to school early to help the freshmen move in. Some of them sign up to be orientation leaders for the sole purpose of meeting the new freshmen.

110 >> Public Address

Staff members at Lawrence Tech University have received permission from the school administration to address the freshmen orientation groups. A student is allowed to explain the ministry of Campus Crusade during this time.

111 >> Class Unity

At the spring retreat at Indiana University, staff members pit the classes against each other in competition, class against class. The winning class gets a pizza party.

112 >> Getting to Know You

At Northwestern, Campus Crusade conducts registration line surveys of all incoming freshmen. Despite the fact that freshmen start a week before everyone else, Campus Crusade

students return early to help the freshmen move in. They also hand out printed invitations to an off-campus party. They have done this for three years and every year it gets bigger and bigger. It's a great way to get to know believers and non-believers.

113 >> Move-in Day

On freshmen move-in day, returning students at Indiana University help the new ones move in to their dorms. About 100 students will divide up, all wearing the same T-shirt, and head to the dorms to help the freshmen move in. They hand the new students a flyer that advertises Campus Crusade.

114 >> Traditional Surveys Work

Traditional surveys work well in the fall for Ohio University. On the first day of classes, all of the questionnaires are put in a database and the Campus Crusade students knock on the door of every single Bible study contact. Their goal is to follow-up with every person expressing interest in a Bible study within the first nine days of school.

115 >> "3 on 6"

At Brown University, three upper-class students involved with the ministry are given the names of six freshmen who were contacts from earlier outreaches. With three students all sharing responsibility for the same six, it is less likely that one might "fall through the cracks." The plan is to demonstrate genuine care for the freshmen and to reach out to them.

116 ›› Dorm Life

Staff members at Montana University encourage their students to move back in the dorms so they can meet the freshmen. Campus Crusade students are trained to think strategically about how to reach everyone in their dorm, and how to build relationships with the residents. As a matter of spiritual encouragement and to emphasize the seriousness of this sacrifice, the staff members commission the upperclassmen before they move into the dorms.

117 ›› "Is There A God?"

The University of Montana sent mailings into the freshmen dorms that included the ESC article, "Is There A God?" along with coupons from local businesses. Comment cards were also used so the students could mail them back to Campus Crusade. No postage was necessary since they were using campus mail.

118 ›› Great Race

Rafting provides an opportunity for team building at the University of Oregon. Staff members try to gather the freshmen to go to the McKenzie River for a rafting competition. It's a great way for the students to work as a team and to start building relationships.

119 ›› Branding

The staff members at Penn State University wanted to create an effective brand for Campus Crusade. They hired a graphic design firm who designed a logo, used in conjunction with black and white photos. They also created a five-minute video and sent postcards advertising the video to the homes of incoming freshmen. When they arrived on campus, the video was waiting in their mailboxes. Billboards were posted across campus and ads were put in a magazine that the freshmen read.

120 ›› Dinner Giveaways

During the first week of school at the University of Virginia, Frisbees, stadium cups, water bottles, and mini footballs are given out in the dinner line. Campus Crusade students conduct one-minute questionnaires and then do follow-up.

121 ›› Crusade Cook-out

Campus Crusade at Eastern Kentucky created a partnership with the university during freshman orientation to host a cookout. The university pays for the cookout and Campus Crusade students come back early to help the new freshman move in, to serve the food at the cookout, and to run the music. (For returning students, it's promoted as a mini-missions trip.) Comment cards are handed out at the beginning of every food line asking students if they are interested in being in a Bible study.

122 ›› Freshman Retreat

Campus Crusade at UNC, Chapel Hill hosts a freshman retreat. On the first weekend of the school year, everyone gathers for fun and to hear several talks on having a healthy college life. The seniors return a day early and are very intentional about connecting with the new freshman.

DAMAH

SPIRITUAL EXPERIENCES IN FILM

Reaching every stu-
dent with the gospel
includes engaging
students at every
point in their spiritual journey.
The Damah Film Festival: Spiritual Experiences in Film is one
attempt to connect with students
who are early in this journey
and who have little desire to
interact with Christians.

Although not a ministry of Campus
Crusade, Damah has produced several
tools we can use on campus. For the
last couple years they have encouraged filmmakers of all skill levels to tell
stories that capture raw, truthful mo-
ments of spiritual redemption, struggle,
inspiration, or surprise. The result is
a collection of eloquently told stories
from many perspectives that challenge
students to consider the spiritual side of
life. The last two years they've received
over 300 submissions and screened
approximately 150 films at their annual
3-day festival in Seattle.

> For the last couple years they have encouraged filmmakers of all skill levels to tell stories that capture raw, truthful moments of spiritual redemption, struggle, inspiration, or surprise.

We've all known for years that the emerging generation is heavily influenced by entertainment media and deeply moved by the power of story. Damah offers two DVDs, each with 10-15 stories as well as a touring festival that can be tailored to an individual campus' needs. Each story, chosen for its ability to raise a legitimate spiritual issue or question, can reach into a student's life, touch their emotions and produce a greater willingness to reveal what's going on inside. This "teams" well with some of our other approaches that engage the mind more than the emotions. Because the films have a variety of perspectives, students with false perceptions of Christianity have the freedom to interact with us.

How can you use them? Here are a few ideas to spur your thinking:

Individually:
Stories on the DVD and the Damah Web site deal with themes of grace, God's Sovereignty, misconceptions of Jesus, favor with God, the need to worship something, and many other topics. Send students to the site or loan them the DVD to watch a single film that's pertinent to an issue in their lives.

Small Groups:
Have students host a study break on their dorm floor once a week where they view a 10-minute film and discuss it for 20-30 minutes. Simply listening to the discussion will produce uncanny insight into the lives of those that they've been praying for.

Use selected films as a discussion starter for the 7 themes of Life@Large.

After a couple weeks of viewing spiritual stories together have students begin to share their own spiritual story.

Large Groups / Campus-Wide Events
Host a Damah Touring Festival on campus tailored to your specific needs. Because Damah is not perceived as a Christian event, you might partner with the film department or the inter-faith council and have them help cover costs. Work ahead of time with your students to help them understand the themes in the film and questions to ask. It's a great way to offer something compelling to the campus community while opening a plethora of opportunity for discussions on the spiritual nature of life to start all over campus. *

123» Investigating God

This year, UC Davis tried GIGs (Groups Investigating God, an evangelistic Bible study developed by Intervarsity Christian Fellowship). Figures show that GIGs are becoming effective in giving students the opportunity to discover Jesus in a safe community. Many students have come to Christ in this relational style, evangelistic small group. To learn more about GIGs and to order the Bible study series, visit www.gospelcom.net/cgi-ivpress/book.pl/code=2024/.

124» Cup and Coke

For the first six weeks of classes, Iowa State University focuses on the freshman. One way they do that is by printing 2,500 plastic cups that have the football schedule on one side of them. They stick a soda can inside and pass them out with a spiritual interest survey.

125» Letter of Encouragement

The Milwaukee Metro team connects with the new freshmen through the Christian faculty on campus. Staff members send them letters on behalf of the faculty. The letter asks how their first year of school is going and lets them know that someone will be stopping by to see how they're doing and to drop off a helpful book, "More Than A Carpenter." When a staff member visits a student, they go through a freshman survey with them and ask if they're interested in hearing about the gospel.

126» Stout Socials

UW, Stout hosts a freshmen ice-cream social-the invitation comes with a plastic spoon tied to it. The event isn't particularly evangelistic, but it does gather freshmen. In addition, Stout has bonfires and cookouts at apartment complexes and many students that go are freshmen.

127» Professors and Planners

Campus Crusade at Texas A&M use the Christian professors to distribute freshmen planners. The angle is that the students are receiving them from someone that they respect.

128» Prep Work

The San Antonio Metro team created a college prep seminar aimed at graduating high-school seniors. The seminars use multi-media and humor to help seniors understand the realities of college. Seniors enjoy the College Prep Seminars for their wise insights, biblical challenge and creative presentation. For more information, visit www.collegeprep.org.

129» Interactive CD

Staff at Southwest Missouri State put together an interactive CD that included video clips of meetings, Bible studies, the gospel of John,

Life@Large, and the Four Spiritual Laws. For three years, they have distributed the CDs, totaling around 4,000. They created a perception among students that Campus Crusade is a "cutting-edge," even trendy, group. However, the students weren't viewing the CDs, and so next year they plan to pass out student planners.

FRINGE GROUPS››

130›› Building Bridges

At the University of Wisconsin in Madison, Campus Crusade hosted an Easter debate between a Christian and an atheist. The topic was the resurrection of Jesus and the event took place in the middle of campus. To build further bridges to the atheist club, students from Campus Crusade play paintball with the group.

131›› Connecting with Diverse Groups

Baltimore Metro has looked for ways to connect with other groups on campus. They have found that doing service projects together is a helpful way to form relationships. On one of their campuses, they teamed up with a homosexual group to run a food drive. Through the project, the students got a chance to know the Christians and some even attended a Bible study. The two groups got to know each other in a non-threatening environment. Some of the students from the other group had been raised in church and were interested in checking out what Campus Crusade was about.

132›› Alternative Evangelism

At Ball State University, various students have been attending the gay/lesbian club. One of Campus Crusade's student leaders went regularly to the club and was nominated to be an officer. However, he hadn't told anybody that he was a Christian. He wasn't elected. In addition, Bible studies have popped up in the theatre, dance and music departments. It has been a great way to reach out to those living alternative lifestyles.

133›› Deliverance

At Baldwin Wallace, a student who lives in a majority homosexual dorm started a group called "Deliverance." The topics have included homosexuality and eating disorders. The group has been seeing 11 attend each week with a total of 20 students walking through the door. All those attending have been non-Christians.

134›› March On

At the University of Colorado, Boulder, Campus Crusade has joined the gay/lesbian students in their marches as a way to show that they don't have hateful feelings toward them.

135›› Set Free

At Central Washington University, the gay/lesbian club performs a gay wedding every year during abstinence week. This year, Campus Crusade brought in Bob Blackford to share his testimony of contracting HIV through homosexuality. Bob shared to a packed house how God set him free from the homosexual lifestyle.

136›› Searching

When Iowa State did the "I Agree With" campaign, the president of the Atheist club began to attend Campus Crusade's weekly meeting. Relationships were being built between the two groups and the treasurer of the Atheist club also started attending Bible study.

University of Minnestota

THE ATHEISTS &
HUMANISTS CLUB

FROM SCOTT MATHEWS

> "Sure we're curious about the lecture, but mostly we are here to thank Charlie for the doughnuts and the invitation."

When Charlie, a Christian, walked into the Atheists and Humanists Club meeting at the University of Minnesota, he wanted to extend an olive branch to the group. So, with a box of doughnuts in hand, he introduced himself and said, "I'm a Christian and I'm involved with Campus Crusade for Christ." Then Charlie invited the 13 club members to an assembly with prominent Christian chemist Dr. Fritz Schaeffer called "Christianity and Science: Friend or Foe."

More than 400 students attended Schaeffer's presentation-plus all 13 students from the Atheists and Humanists Club!

One member of the Atheist club said, "Sure we're curious about the lecture, but mostly we are here to thank Charlie for the doughnuts and the invitation."

Charlie asked the club members to complete a five-question spiritual interest survey. The last question on the survey read: "If you rated all your desires on a scale from 1-10, with those things you desire most being a 10 and the things you desire least being a 1, where would you put your desire to know God?"

Four of them wrote the number 10, one wrote 8, and another wrote 7. Only 5 of the 13 expressed no interest. ✱

Beginning a Ministry in a Fraternity or Sorority

BY ISAAC JENKINS

(Excerpt taken from the book "Becoming an insider in Greek ministry")

Fraternities and Sororities are one of the most strategic places to invest your time in ministry. Here are some ideas to get you started.

Longevity

The degree of ministry success in a fraternity or sorority will correspond to the span of time you spend laboring there. Strategies and methods are important but it often takes three to four years to see real fruit.

Getting started

Start by targeting the three top fraternities or sororities. My first goal is

> The degree of ministry success in a fraternity or sorority will correspond to the span of time you spend laboring there.

to start a coed Bible study with two or three pledge classes. Ask the girls which fraternity pledge class they would like to invite over for a coed study. Always have the study at the sorority as some girls feel intimidated walking into a fraternity.

Meet the Pledge Trainer

Always meet the Chapter's pledge trainer early on. Talk with them face to face so they know you are a normal person. Go by the house during lunchtime so you can sit and talk.

Most need speakers to fill their weekly pledge meetings. I offer talks on time management, making wise decisions and setting goals. Recently, a two-part talk on manhood has gone over so well that I doubt I will ever speak on anything else.

Starting a Bible study: Freshmen

It is imperative that you hold the study at a time convenient for them. I have found that before dinner, early in the week, at their house, is a good time. Later in the week is not good because many are looking ahead to the weekend.

Bible Study Ideas

There is really no "magic" study that is "THE" answer to reaching Greeks. Campus Crusade and Christian bookstores are full of good ideas. Some of the best studies I have led are simply studies where I have walked a group through a book that they were interested in. Model openness and they will open up to you.

Evangelism with Freshmen

Do the bulk of your evangelism in the fall, when you have the opportunity to meet with more guys and spend time with new believers. The second semester is when I focus on discipling new believers. Grow your ministry in the first semester, build into it in the second semester.

Evangelism With Upper Classmen

Befriend the actives as well. As I develop a relationship with a few guys and begin a house study, I then follow up each new active and share Christ with him. *

*For more information and resources about working with Greeks, check out: 4greeks.org

GREEK STUDENTS››

138›› The Dating Game

Welcome to the Dating Game at Stephen F. Austin University. Four guys from four houses participated in the game. Their friends came to cheer them on. A total of 80 sorority women and 70 fraternity men attended. One guy and one girl emceed the event. The bachelorette was a sharp Campus Crusade, sorority girl and the event was hosted in her sorority house. The winner got a double date with her and a staff couple. Contact cards were used, but there was more of a response from the women. A short, 15-minute talk was given on relationships. Announcements were made the week before the event in each of the Greek houses. The announcement indicated that there would be a short talk after the event.

139›› Greek Game

Arkansas Metro hosts a fun game for the new pledge classes each year. Around 60-100 students participate. A sorority and fraternity president will each go up to the front and are asked five questions that are fun ice-breakers. Then, everyone breaks up into small groups to discuss different questions.

140›› Spreading the Word

The Chicago Metro team distributes brochures to all the Greek houses. The brochures are targeted for the presidents and share about the different talks that Campus Crusade offers that will assist Greek students with their spiritual lives, their grades, and living with a purpose.

141›› Cokes and Greeks

Michigan State uses coke surveys with the Greek students. They ask them, "Do you want to get together and get a coke and talk about spiritual things?" They also utilize a local police officer who is a former Campus Crusade staff member. He is a chapter advisor for one of the fraternities and speaks a lot on risk management.

142›› Greek Day

Southwest Missouri State hosts a "Greek Day" as a way to thank the Greeks for their community service. Campus Crusade helps out with the event where there is a guest speaker who usually ends up sharing the gospel.

143›› Testimonial

At the University of Virginia, a student who had struggled with alcoholism shared about his battle and his faith in a fraternity house. Thirty men attended the outreach and ten were interested in meeting with someone.

144›› Greek Cookout

At Eastern Kentucky, Campus Crusade hosts a Greek cookout where they invite Greek presidents and ask them to bring their chapters. Around 400 come each year and some of them use it as a philanthropy event and bring canned foods. Staff members distribute Greek planners and a few students share about the weekly meeting and how to get involved with the ministry.

145›› Greek Serenades

In Milwaukee, Campus Crusade enjoys hosting a Christmas program for the sororities each year. The guys' role is to serenade the women with different Christmas carols. The singing and dancing progressively gets goofier, and then they transition into something more formal and sing a more polished song that really blesses the women. They also leave a basket of candy along with an encouraging Bible verse. This is done year after year so that when these students connect with Campus Crusade again, they might be more inclined to become involved.

146>> All Greek Mixer

There had never been an all-Greek freshmen mixer at Texas Christian University until Campus Crusade got involved. The staff helped to sponsor the first one on campus. Each fraternity initiated with a sorority to escort them to the event. Pizza was donated and a fun, five-minute survey was conducted with the students in the end.

147>> Rock-A-Thon

At Towson University, one of the members of the Alpha Gamma Delta sorority was injured in a car wreck. She was also involved with the ministry so Campus Crusade partnered with her sorority to host the Rock-A-Thon, a community event that was used to raise money for the girl's expenses.

INTERNATIONAL STUDENTS>>

148>> Home and the Meaning of Christmas

by Kimberly McCarty, JMU

What better place to reach out to international students at Christmastime than your home? Staff member Kimberly McCarty and her church worked together to host three Christ-themed parties for 17 students from countries like Holland, China, Latvia, Mexico, Ecuador, Yugoslavia, Nigeria, and Bulgaria.

Her church provided the guest speakers and the refreshments. Two speakers told the Christmas story using the nativity and another speaker used a Christmas tree prop, outlining the gospel with the ornaments on the tree.

Everyone also made a craft (called a Christingle, originally from Marienborn, Germany), lit candles and sang "Silent Night" and "Joy to the World." At the close, each student received a gift-wrapped *JESUS* film DVD with an ornament attached to the package.

149>> Coffee House builds bridges

To reach international students in the Seattle area, Campus Crusade opened a weekly coffeehouse, open just before or after the weekly Campus Crusade meeting. There is no program, just a room filled with coffee makers, snacks, and music. A perfect environment for conversations to happen between the Campus Crusade students and the international students they know.

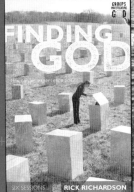

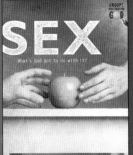

150›› Thanksgiving with International Students

International students can find themselves alone during Thanksgiving week. One staff couple at East Tennessee State sponsored a Thanksgiving meal for international students. The couple's church graciously provided the food and the extra amenities.

151›› International Fashion Show

International students often miss their home country and their culture while studying here in America. Campus Crusade at East Tennessee State saw an opportunity to connect with international students and allow them to share their cultures with each other. In a partnership with a campus international organization, Campus Crusade staff members and students helped organize an international fashion show. International students wore their cultural dresses, and explained a little about their countries. The fashion show also allowed Campus Crusade students to show their interest in other cultures.

152›› World Religion's Panel

A World Religion's Panel was organized at the University of Oklahoma in conjunction with the Hindu, Muslim, and Jewish groups on campus. Only the Buddhist group chose not to participate. The goal was to highlight four questions and the corresponding answers from each religion.

At the catered event, people were assigned tables and provided a list of guided questions. Trained students sat at each table to help explain Christianity and to begin building relationships with the international students.

153›› Talk Time

The ministry at Central Washington has a specific focus on international students. They help them practice English through "Talk Time," and host social activities like progressive dinners.

154›› Planet Partners

University of Mississippi staff members encourage their students to get involved with the "planet partners" program. This university-sponsored program provides an easy link with an international student on campus.

155›› Japanese Focus

UC Santa Barbara customized their FSs fo Japanese students.

156›› Where's Your Focus?

At Dickinson State University, staff members encourage a focus on reaching the Chinese and Japanese students. They've given away Chinese and Japanese Bibles, as well as the JESUS film, and they've watched the film with the students.

157›› Center of English as a Second Language

You may not have to look beyond your own campus to find strategic partners in ministry. The students at the University of Oklahoma sought out the Center for English as a Second Language, offering to help international students learn English.

158›› Using the JESUS film on campus

Imagine being in a country that doesn't speak your native language and yet being able to watch a video in your own language.

THE_ORACLE

i see. i see stuff. i know all kinds of things. i'm kinda like a giant eyeball.
yeah, that's it. in some ways i'm kinda like a big, giant eyeball.
i stare into the abyss of www.allspiritualknowledge and find the meaning of life.
i'm a bit blood shot, but still smarter than you.
i am the _oracle.

 **478 websites, 87 articles, 42 videos**
films, music, games, and other odd stuff
(a different approach to evangelism)

step into the world of the_oracle

 As I turn, I see and learn.

"Nick joined the cricket club!"

159 ››

Minnestota State University
CRICKET MINISTRY

BY PAUL SCHOLTEN

Nick, a student involved in the campus ministry at Minnesota State University- Mankato, had a great ministry idea while watching the cricket club do a half time demonstration at a basketball game. Nick noticed that all the players were from Middle Eastern descent-students he doesn't connect with day to day.

So, Nick joined the cricket club! As Nick has learned, Middle Eastern cultures values relationships. As he builds friendships with these men, Nick can share with them what God means to him. *

Campus Crusade at the University of Oklahoma researched the demographics of international students and freely provided them with JESUS films in their native tongues. To receive a copy of the film, the students had to sign a card to indicate the specific language and could check off, "I'd be willing to give my feedback on the film."

160 ›› **Reaching International Families**
Campus Crusade at Southern Methodist University sought to reach out to the international families. They hosted an Easter event, inviting the wives and children of international students. They offered an arts and crafts time for the kids, explained the meaning of Easter, and then showed the JESUS film.

161 ›› **International Kits**
Michigan State is a campus with large numbers of international undergraduates. To reach these students, Campus Crusade put together International Kits and passed them out. A local church paid for the kits and local businesses provided coupons. A survey was included asking the international student if

he/she wanted to get together with someone who would help them learn English or who would take them to get groceries. This idea also worked well with churches that wanted to pair international students with host families.

162 >> A Holistic Approach

A few students at UW LaCrosse have moved into the International Hall with the intention of building relationships with the international students.

In addition to sharing life with the international students, FSKs were given out along with a booklet called "How to survive in the US." Bible studies were also hosted within the hall.

MEN>>

163 >> A Time To Get Away

Twin City Metro took a retreat away from campus as a way to focus on the men. They actually went to an AIDS camp where there was a need for some construction work to be done. The men stayed at the camp for a whole weekend. They divided their time between working at the camp, listening to some talks, and having some fun. The retreat was successful in getting the guys into a new environment where they could work together and get to know each other better.

164 >> Pulling An All-Nighter

At the University of Florida, Campus Crusade rented out a gym and opened it up for an all night event. There was a good blend of activity, content, and food. There was a basketball tournament and then times out for lessons on David or manhood.

165 >> Final Four Outreach

At the University of Wisconsin, Oshkosh, Campus Crusade hosted a Final Four outreach. Articles were handed out about the Final Four and everyone on campus was invited. A football player gave his testimony during halftime and a DVD player was given away at the end.

WOMEN>>

166 >> Stanford Speaker

At Stanford, Campus Crusade utilized a student who had struggled with an eating disorder her freshman year. By the time the girl was a senior, she had developed a dorm program. After giving her program, she encouraged the girls to join a four-week investigative study. In the future, the staff plan to partner with the Women's Center to host similar programs.

167 >> A Vision for Athletes

Part of the vision statement of Campus Crusade at Southern Methodist University is to reach every part of campus. The staff women were asked to each target an athletic team. They were to initiate time with the coaches, the students, and to set up a chaplain time. One hundred AIA magazines were ordered for the soccer, golf, swim, and rowing teams. Strategies used were ordering Michele Ackers' book for the soccer team, breakfasts after swim practice, a talk on taking care of every area of your life (physical, mental, and spiritual) and personal testimonies.

168 >> Freshman Fashion Show

At Southern Methodist University, Campus Crusade wants to be seen as an informed ministry and relevant in the eyes of the world. To target the needs of some of the young women,

Campus Crusade began hosting a fashion show for those going through Rush. 750 invitations were sent out and 350 women attended.

Dessert was donated by a bakery and coffee by Starbucks. The clothes were also donated from stores including Ann Taylor and Kenneth Cole. The models were all young women involved in Campus Crusade Bible studies. Former Miss Arizona, Stacey Kole, spoke and tailored her talk around sorority Rush. The young women got the feeling that Campus Crusade understood what they were going through and that they wanted to help prepare them for it.

Every girl attending the show received a FSK that was customized for the fashion show. The guys got involved behind the scenes by helping to set up and by serving the beverages. Now, Campus Crusade is partnering with Panhellenic to host the fashion show. Flyers are sent out to advertise the show and it's put on the school calendar. The styles worn during the fashion show are posted on the local ministry's web page as well as the testimonies of four sorority women who received Christ.

169 ›› To Pledge or Not to Pledge

"To Pledge or Not to Pledge" is an evangelistic dorm program for young women at Baylor University. This program attracts the girls who are thinking about pledging a sorority. One sorority woman and one non-sorority woman share their different points of view. The program ends with a talk that challenges the young women to think about what their hope is really in.

170 ›› Conversation and Cuisine

One female staff member at Baylor University runs a ministry home for girls. She opens her home to young women involved with Campus Crusade and they use it to host outreaches. The girls invite their non-Christian friends to dinner every month. The staff member reminds them in advance that they're responsible for bringing a friend who needs to hear about God. After dinner, the staff member shares a salty nugget from the Word. She got the idea from the book, "Conversation and Cuisine" which talks about food and how to reach out to those who need to hear the gospel.

171 ›› Dating 101

During the first semester at Baylor, female Campus Crusade staff target the girls through "Dating 101," an evangelistic talk on relationships. The girls all gather in a female staff member's home and she shares about the "crush cycle" and how to get out of a crush. The gospel isn't shared during the program, but it opens the door for later opportunities.

172 ›› Mary Kay Makeovers

At Elmhurst, the Chicago Metro team hosts a Mary Kay outreach where they offer free makeovers. They invite non-believers from the dorms. One of the staff members does a talk on beauty and girls are followed-up through comment cards.

173 ›› Wedding Outreach

At the University of Toledo, Campus Crusade knows what subject will attract a crowd of young women. All of the women are invited to hear about how to plan an inexpensive wedding and what to look for in a husband.

174 ›› Greek Alumni Reach Out to Sorority

At Ball State University, Campus Crusade is taking advantage of Greek alumni. With one sorority in particular, the wife of a former congressman is an alumni. She and her husband opened up their home to a few sorority girls and cooked them dinner. Afterwards the alumni shared their testimony.

Texas Tech
MINSTERING TO WOMEN

BY KATHERINE HILL

> I've been to many programs, but I have never seen so many women attend.

Women on campus today will either be struggling with an eating disorder or know a friend who is struggling with an eating disorder. In order to address this issue and communicate the gospel we brought in Stacey Kole last February. Stacy spoke regarding the facts and issues surrounding eating disorders and then interjected a brief 5-minute testimony of how she overcame her disorder through a personal relationship with Jesus Christ.

Student Life and Panhellenic co-sponsored the event with us. Most of my ideas of how to market the event came through learning about how the campus advertises for events and from how Tech advertises for Body Awareness Week.

We blitzed the campus by putting banners on all buses on campus, sent letters to all human sciences, psychology,

food and nutrition and family studies departments asking for professors to give extra credit to their students for attending the event. We sent a postcard to every woman on campus which involved getting a mailing list from campus, purchasing the labels, and we spent $160 to mail the postcards. Some of the sororities made the program mandatory and some were able to earn Greek week points for attending.

It was all worth it to see 600 women attend, and 346 fill out comment cards with 151 indicating a request for more information about a relationship with God. The President of Panhellenic said, "I've been to many programs, but I have never seen so many women attend." We were able to follow up the next morning at a coffee shop for Q&A with staff and other ministries on campus. Stacy visited 10 sororities so the women could interact with her and we went to dinner that night with the Panhellenic group. *

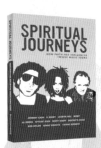
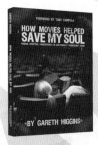

176 ›› Crusade Coffee House

Campus Crusade students at Indiana University hosted a coffee house in a dorm. They brought in a mother who shared her experience in dealing with tragedy. There was free coffee from Starbucks and desserts.

177 ›› Sharing with Student Moms

At the University of New Mexico, one of the staff mothers hosts a mom's group for student moms and over half are non-believers.

178 ›› Spa Parties

At Iowa State University, Campus Crusade invested in paraffin wax machines and hosted spa parties as a way to gather young women. They set up the wax and massage oil and allow 45 minutes for the women to enjoy some time of relaxation and relationship building. Then, a staff woman gives a talk on the way women view themselves and the way God views them.

179 ›› The Meaning of Beauty

"Inner Beauty, Outer Beauty" is a strategy used by the Milwaukee Metro team. They use Mary Kay cosmetics and give the girls a makeover. The gospel is shared at the end.

180 ›› Christmas Tea

Christmas is a natural opportunity to talk about Christ and for the third year in a row, the staff women at Indiana University have hosted Christmas Teas to talk about the season's true meaning. This year, three separate teas were held--one especially for Greek women.

At the tea, staff member Sadee Connors explained how God gave the first Christmas gift ever-His son Jesus Christ. About five women accepted Christ both this year and last year.

"What a joy it was to have one of my Alpha Phi sisters become a sister in Christ that night," Sadee said. "A student involved in our ministry has been praying for Alpha Phi for two and a half years."

181 ›› Taking A Break

Christmas study breaks have worked well in the past for the University of Wisconsin, Oshkosh. Campus Crusade invites the women on a dorm floor and everyone shares their Christmas traditions. Someone also shares the real meaning of Christmas and then there is an invitation to receive Christ. They have seen 10-15 women trust Christ each year.

innovation
center for technology

Ninety-two percent of college freshmen are wired and use the Internet daily

to gather academic information, class notes, and even take tests. In a recent survey, 100% said they share music and other items of interest from the Internet. Over 70 million songs are swapped, along with 350 thousand full-length movies every single day! Can you see the possibilities?

A large percentage of this energy is made up of people looking for something to fill idle time or relieve the stress of life. To others it has become an addiction to escape into a fantasy world. The battle for the minds and souls of people is sometimes won or lost in cyberspace.

> **"Students are looking for insight in the privacy and convenience of the Internet. We just have to point them where to look.** "

The Campus Ministry, understanding this, has mobilized entirely new strategies and tools to effectively engage in the spiritual battle taking place on the Internet. The Innovation Center for Technology is designed to communicate the gospel and answers to life's most crucial questions for those who are searching for something.

Maybe they want to know God. Maybe they just want to know if heaven is really there, or how can they get over their guilt and pain, or maybe they just want to know why Christians think they've cornered the market on religion. Students are looking for insight in the privacy and convenience of the Internet. We just have to point them to where to look. Several sites open the possibilities of turning lost students into Christ-centered laborers including www.EveryStudent.com and www.JoePix.com.

This year several campuses have made EveryStudent.com a key part of their evangelistic strategy. And the results have been very encouraging. From August 2002 - April 2003, a total of 160,300 students visited the site and 2,636 indicated that they received Christ. For free down-loadable materials and information on how to use the EveryStudent.com strategy, visit www.escmedia.com.

JoePix is a photo evangelism(tm) strategy that mobilizes students at major campus events to engage their peers with the gift of a free digital photo and an invitation to retrieve it from the JoePix outreach website. At Big Break 2003, our students took photos of 17,052 people in eight days. 63% of those photos were retrieved and likely viewed and each time a student retrieves a photo they are given an opportunity to explore the Big Picture, that is, the Gospel. We are making plans to run a JoePix evangelistic outreach on 50 campuses this fall. For information or scheduling please contact JoePix@innovationctr.com.

At the Innovation Center, our goal is reach out to lost students and help our staff and students in their ministry by moving the Internet into the center of ministry. ✳

For information on how you and your students can leverage technology, please contact Chris.Willard@innovationctr.com

PLEASE SUBSCRIBE!

If you wish to recieve the next issue of the Journal.

You should have already received your complimentary first issue, and we hope you've found it a scrumptious ministry tool. Every semester we hope to gather the best field-born ideas, tools, and resources on a different topic and distribute it to you on a CD.

Upcoming Journal topics will probably include:

- ◆ What all staff can learn from catalytic ministry
- ◆ Communicating the ministry of the Holy Spirit
- ◆ New approaches to evangelism
- ◆ Apples, are they really nature's toothbrush?

Then again, who knows. We may do a different topic if something comes up that seems more interesting to us and more helpful to you.

These things aren't cheap to make and mail, and there's not a cent of profit margin, so please subscribe so we have the money to produce the next Journal.

To subscribe go to:
http://centerfieldproductions.com

OR FILL OUT THE BOTTOM AND SEND TO:

XXXXXXXXXXXXXXXXXXXXXXXXXXXXXXXXXXXXXXXXXXXXXXX

CENTERFIELD PRODUCTIONS
513 N. Franklin St.
West Chester, PA 19380

NAME:_____

email:_____ ACCT. #_____

A Miscellany

CHURCH PARTNERSHIPS

182 ›› You Are Our Campus Ministry

Every local movement dreams to hear those words. UNC - Chapel Hill has a great partnership with two neighboring churches. One church gives $9,000 every year to the campus ministry. Many of the students attend these churches and Campus Crusade often invites the pastors as guest speakers for the weekly meeting. The leaders of the churches appreciate the ministry skills that Campus Crusade provides to the students. To help seniors transition into the workplace, Campus Crusade invites lay people from the churches to speak about transitioning their faith into the workplace and service in the church.

183 ›› Adopt a Campus

San Antonio Metro realizes that they cannot reach their scope of 80,000 students on 12 different campuses unless they form partnerships with the surrounding churches. Campus Crusade in San Antonio has the vision to see a church partner for every campus to help reach every college student. In exchange for a church partnership, Campus Crusade will provide the resources and train the volunteers. John Allert, the metro director, has developed material on how to establish church partnerships and how to train volunteers.

184 ›› Church Takes Care of Campus Website

A church in Tulsa, Oklahoma created and paid for the design of the Campus Crusade Website for the University of Louisiana, Lafayette. The ministry did not have the resources to design a website so the church provided for this need. A local church in town has also partnered with Campus Crusade by helping support students to conferences and occasionally helping with babysitting needs at conferences.

185 ›› Volunteers Help Follow-Up Surveys

George Mason University has partnered with a local church to provide volunteers to help follow-up surveys. These volunteers are young business professionals who come on campus during the evenings early in the school year. They meet on campus for pizza before visiting the students. Afterwards the group takes time to debrief. Commuter students make up 85% of George Mason's student body. They have found that a businessperson can meet with commuter students more easily than the staff could.

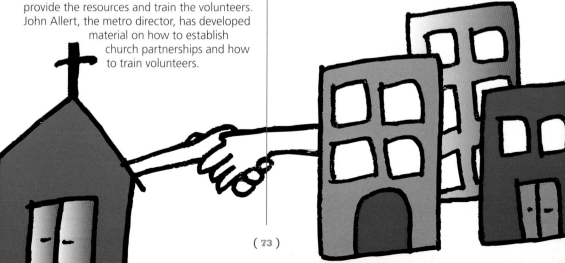

University of Wisconsin - Oshkosh

TRUE LOVE

SARA THOMPSON

> "The men and women both love it and the comment cards were incredibly positive!"

Having plans on Valentines Day is a

must. So every year, the movement at the University of Wisconsin-Oshkosh hosts an elegant Valentines Day dessert to talk about true love from God's perspective.

The women receive formal invitations and then are given flowers when the guys pick them up. Later, the catered evening has the men taking orders and doing all the serving.

Tables are decorated with candles and rose petals, lights are dimmed and Frank Sinatra plays in the background. On the screen, Bible verses on love fade in and out. Later, a student tells how God changed her heart toward dating and how her significance is now with God, and not with men.

Continuing with the program, a song is performed, and a guest speaker talks about the true love found in Jesus Christ. Twelve girls accepted Christ! Meanwhile, in another room, the men listened to a message on caring for their sisters in Christ.

"It is good for everyone and incredibly successful," says Sara Thompson. "The men and women both love it and the comment cards were incredibly positive!" *

Autumn

187 ›› Pumpkin Outreach

At South Dakota State, hundreds of pumpkins were donated to Campus Crusade. In exchange for completing a spiritual interest survey, students received a free pumpkin, and in one morning, every pumpkin was given away. Students also received a quarter page evangelistic article that compared people to the jack-o-lantern.

188 》》 Reverse Trick or Treating

At Charlotte Metro, Campus Crusade students did a Reverse Trick or Treating as a way to talk with students. Stopping by different rooms, they gave away candy and FSKs.

189 》》 Satanism and the Occult

Around Halloween, students in Chicago did a talk on Satanism and the occult. They also handed out candy and had students fill out a Halloween survey.

190 》》 Thanksgiving Postcards

At Rutgers University, Campus Crusade delivered free Thanksgiving postcards through campus mail. With turkeys on the front side, students wrote notes to friends on the backside. As students would fill out the postcard, Campus Crusade staff members or students asked questions like "What are you thankful for?" Other times, they just wanted to expose people to the ministry's presence on campus, explaining, "We're not asking you for anything. We just want to deliver these cards for you."

Winter

191 》》 A Candy Cane for Every Student

The students at the University of South Dakota bought candy canes from Sam's Club and put them in student's mailboxes along with an evangelistic article.

192 》》 Apartment Visits

For Christmas, Campus Crusade at Mississippi State went to apartments where they knew students lived. Going door-to-door they gave away candy canes, Christmas cards, and selected material from FSKs. During Easter, they distributed Easter baskets, including in each one a copy of "More than a Carpenter."

193 》》 Christmas party in my dorm

At Eastern Kentucky, a student hosted a Christmas party in her dorm. Appetizers were served and holiday music played in the background. DVD players were given away and one girl explained what Christmas means to her. Approximately 125 students visited the party, and every student received a copy of Max Lucado's book, "He Chose the Nails."

Other students on campus raised money to give out "More than a Carpenter" as Christmas presents to those living in their dormitory.

194 》》 Love Survey

For a Valentine's Day outreach, the students in Jacksonville downloaded a love survey off of the GodSquad.com Web site. They also displayed a huge board on campus that read, "Does Love Truly Satisfy?"

195 》》 Table For Two

At Southern Oregon University, Campus Crusade developed an ESC Valentine's strategy. To enter a drawing for a free dinner-for-two, students filled out a card listing their name and address. In exchange, each one received the ESC article, "Sex and the Search for Intimacy."

196 》》 Bright Monkey

During Valentine's week, West Virginia students filled out Valentine's Questionnaires to win a huge stuffed monkey. Campus Crusade raffled off a stuffed animal for each dorm. The bright monkey was sure to draw attention to the table. Staff members said the stuffed animals were actually cheaper than buying candy.

197 》》 A Rose For Every Girl

For Valentine's Day, Campus Crusade at Appalachian State placed a rose on every girl's dorm room door and followed-up with focus groups. Approximately 2,600 roses were distributed.

UT Knoxville also gave away 1500 flowers on Valentine's Day. Cards were given with 12 sentences on the worth of a woman as well as a web address for an article about dating.

198 ›› Valentine's Day of Outreach

At East Tennessee State University, Campus Crusade gave away several hundred cups of hot chocolate for Valentines Day and set up a booth where students could make Valentine's cards for loved ones. Students were also invited to a coffeehouse concert later that evening. Following the concert, a student explained the gospel to the audience.

199 ›› Five Love Languages

The ministry in Minnesota State, Mankato, spent two weeks doing surveys aimed at Valentines Day. Based on those results, they hosted an evangelistic meeting on the topic of the Five Love Languages and served "Better Than Sex" cake.

200 ›› Car Smash Outreach

At the University of Northern Colorado, a student organized a car smash outreach. The men had to fill out a Valentine's survey in order to get the chance to smash on the car with a sledgehammer a few times. One of the questions on the survey read: "What does love mean to you?"

Spring

201 ›› St. Patrick's Day Dance

At Boise State, Campus Crusade hosted a dance on St. Patrick's Day. At the dance, a speaker dressed up as a monk shared the message of St. Patrick who lived in A.D. 342.

202 ›› Campus wide Easter Egg Hunt

At Lawrence Tech University, Campus Crusade hid 1,000 plastic Easter eggs all over campus. Inside each plastic egg were pieces of candy and a piece of paper that pointed to EveryStudent.com. Instructions were also given inside the eggs for the students to bring their piece of paper to the weekly meeting where they could win a grand prize. The meaning of Easter was shared during the weekly meeting. Also around campus were ESC Easter posters.

Michigan State partnered with other Christian groups on campus and handed out 16,000 Easter eggs. The gospel message was stuffed inside each Easter egg, along with pieces of candy.

Colorado Boulder stuffed raffle tickets inside their Easter eggs, inviting students to a free dinner. Local businesses donated prizes, including a plane ticket one year and a DVD player last year. Several students spoke of how they met Christ and a guest speaker retold the Easter story.

The "Passion Walk" kicks off the first night. Students reenact the Passion of Christ, beginning with the Lord's Supper and going through the Resurrection. This event takes place on different sites around campus and generates a lot of publicity.

206 >> "Where's the Body?" Campaign

At the University of Idaho, Christian groups partnered together for "Where's the Body?" campaign (similar to I Agree with). Students wore T-shirts emblazoned on the back with the question, "Where's the Body?" On the front of the shirt students printed the inviting words, "Ask me, I know." Additionally, ESC ads were placed in the newspaper daily. The answer to the question, "Where's the Body?" (referring, of course, to Christ's body) came on Friday's paper in an article written by Campus Crusade staff member and author Josh McDowell.

207 >> Easter Outreach Banquet

Campus Crusade at the University of Buffalo hosts a formal Easter banquet every year. Tickets were sold to the other groups on campus. Each year, 50 percent of those who attend are non-believers.

208 >> Easter Week at UTEP

Students involved in Destino at the University of El Paso used the ESC Easter campaign. They created T-shirts. They hosted bands, dramas and break-dancers, and they invited different speakers to discuss relevant topics. Each seminar was intended to reach a different major and some were delivered in Spanish.

203 >> "Hey, don't spit on that guy!"

For Easter, students at Indiana University carried a cross through the campus and erected it in a central location. One of the guys was up on the cross and they had someone begin to mock him and spit on him. A crowd gathered and people reacted to it saying, "Hey, don't spit on that guy!" Flyers announced, "Jesus Christ died for you. What does that mean to you?" The flyers advertised the weekly meeting and an upcoming Easter service at a local church.

204 >> Easter Bunny, Bear, and Pig

At Michigan State, students dress up as the Easter Bunny, a bear, and a pig. Students could get their pictures taken with the characters. Then students passed out cards directing people to the local Web site where they could download their digital photos and also learn more about Campus Crusade. The characters also handed out Easter ads that ran simultaneously in the campus newspaper.

205 >> A "Passion Walk" around campus

Ohio University is on the quarter system, so each quarter the ministry leaders plan an evangelistic outreach. For the spring quarter, they have "Faith Week," completely student-run.

209 ›› International Week

At George Mason, Campus Crusade partnered with a local church to reach international students. They sent "Egg-vitations"-plastic eggs with cards inside inviting internationals to dinner.

210 ›› Come Watch the Trial of Jesus

The students at Cal State, Fresno, acted out the trial of Jesus during the day on campus (free speech area). They invited students to attend the Passion play by handing out plastic Easter eggs containing invitations to the trial of Jesus. Close to 150 students watched the drama.

211 ›› Recliners In the Middle of Campus

Students at the University of Kansas set up recliners and chairs in the middle of campus (free speech area) to invite their peers to watch the JESUS film.

212

West Chester University
JOE MILLIONAIRE

BY CYNTHIA HAGEN

> Incredibly, eight guys wanted more information about God and an Every Student Choice article about relationships!

How can you use the wild popularity of reality TV for outreach?

The movement at West Chester University used the final episode of Joe Millionaire-a TV program where "Joe" squires women who think he's a millionaire-to talk about truth in relationships.

Eighteen students gathered to watch the show, and during commercials they talked about relationships, ultimately addressing the lie of the television show (since Joe really wasn't a millionaire). One student was prepared to share his testimony in response to one of the questions.

Incredibly, eight guys wanted more information about God and an Every Student Choice article about relationships!

"With the extreme popularity of reality/romance television," says staff member Cynthia Hagen, "I think this can be reproduced with future shows." *

213 ›› Invite your friends

Texas Christian University staff members believe that focus groups are effective with new believers. Students new in their faith probably have more non-Christians friends. The staff members ask, "Hey, I would love to know what your friends think." The students are asked to collect six to eight of their friends. TCU says the students enjoy the co-ed groups much better. Students want to talk and they want to be heard.

214 ›› Three weeks and then let's discuss God

Virginia Tech organizes three-week discussion groups (or focus groups). The groups work best when the students initiate. During the first week, they talk about life issues; the second week, they talk about relationships like family life and dating; and the last week, the group discusses spiritual issues.

FOCUS GROUP FUN

Northern Arizona University

BY DAN STILL

> "All we did was listen...
> By the end they were asking
> us what we believed. Talk
> about a receptive audience!"

When clothing brands like Tommy Hilfiger want to learn what's important to young people, they talk to them-with the help of focus groups.

The campus movement at Northern Arizona University used this idea to talk to students in McConnell Hall (a large freshman dorm known for its wild parties and apathy) about life, relationships and religion.

Though RAs at the dorm say it's usually hard to get students to attend any events, twenty-eight students attended the group! The focus group helped students express their beliefs-and they even stayed an hour afterward to continue talking.

"All we did was listen," said staff member Dan Still. "By the end, they were asking us what we believed. Talk about a receptive audience! The groups have been great at beginning positive, constructive dialogue and breaking down Christian stereotypes." Dan also said the RAs were

dying to sponsor and even pay for this program. *

216 ›› Classroom Conversions
It's hard to imagine getting your students back into the classroom. But it's true, says the staff members at Rutgers University. They meet in classrooms to eat pizza and discuss God. The staff members at Rutgers believe focus groups have worked well with catalytic schools.

217 ›› Shhhh. Don't Tell the Christians About Damah
Colorado State University brought the Damah Film Festival to their campus. The person organizing the film showing called the other religious groups on campus and invited them. With the hope of drawing out non-believing students, the festival was not announced at the weekly meeting.

The film showings were held in the DC Bottoms, where the Campus Crusade group usually hosts a coffeehouse. They would watch a film, and then talk about it together. Rather than focusing on right or wrong, the staff

MORE FOCUS GROUP EVANGELISM IDEAS ››

members hoped the open discussion might cause students to consider God.

218 》 Giving Students a Taste of Damah First

The University of Colorado - Boulder teamed up with Campus Crusade to bring the Damah Film Festival to their campus. The festival was located in the same theatre where the Campus Crusade group meets for their weekly meeting. To market Damah, Campus Crusade teamed up with some of the dorm RAs. A Campus Crusade staff member would go on a dorm floor, show one of the films, and then facilitate discussion.

219 》 Class Assignment: Hold an Open Forum

A staff member at Indiana University offers a class for students in apologetics and one of their assignments is to hold an open forum. Students invite other students to the dorm lounge for free pizza and to bring any question they may have.

220 》 Let's Discuss C.S. Lewis And We'll Buy Your Book

Many are familiar with the idea of sending a copy of C.S. Lewis writings to students. But William and Mary added something a little different. The Campus Crusade group sent an invitation to every student in the campus mail for a free copy of C.S. Lewis' book, "Miracles," and an opportunity to discuss the book with others.

221 》 Divide and Conquer with "House Cru"

At Ball State University, the ministry planned one weekly meeting night to divide up and go to ten houses off campus. They called it "House Cru" and each location showed the movie, "Remember the Titans." Afterward, they led a discussion. The desire was to create a non-threatening environment to share with students.

FOOD IDEAS 》

222 》 Root Beer Kegger

Campus Crusade students at Citrus College in Los Angeles held a Beer Kegger...make that a Root Beer Kegger on the main quad. Posters were up all week advertising "Free Beer Kegger - Tuesday, 10-2." The word "root" was written in very small font above the word beer. Tons of students came up for a cold one and were surprised to find out it was root beer, most laughing about it and appreciative of the cold drink. Many Campus Crusade students manned the booth and did surveys. Two local college pastors also came out to minister during the outreach.

223 》 Breakfast dorm outreaches

Wake up! Breakfast is served! The dorms at Florida State do not have dining halls, so Campus Crusade has brought breakfast to the dorms. Casserole, juice, and other breakfast items are served to build relationships with the students. Between 50-60 students have woken up for this outreach. The staff encourage students to build relationships before the breakfast. The students go to their friend's dorm rooms, get them out of bed and invite them to breakfast. Two students will usually share their testimony at the event and while the students are eating down in the lounge they can also fill out surveys.

224 》 500 hamburgers grilled

Campus Crusade at San Bernardino Valley College in LA gave away 500 hamburgers, including fixings, chips, and soda. Along with the grub, the ministry did questionnaires and offered some exposure articles. Students initiated and organized the whole community event. The campus paid for the food and the students did the work. Freshman Survival Kits were handed out, several bands played and the gospel was shared.

225 ›› Food communicates love in Hawaii

At the University of Hawaii, students use food to build relationships. Food communicates love within the culture of Hawaii. After each weekly meeting, students often serve potluck dishes and light foods. When they do have a picnic, it's always a barbeque.

226 ›› Snickers Bar

In Toledo, students used a different approach to get students to the weekly meeting. Students handed out fliers to classmates inviting them to the next Campus Crusade weekly meeting. Attached to the flier is a Snickers bar with the words, "Nothing Satisfies Like Jesus."

227 ›› Pancake night

At the University of New Mexico, a freshmen men's Bible study living in campus apartments decided to turn on the griddle all night and flip pancakes. They didn't advertise; it was just word of mouth. Over 200 students showed up. The party was too big for their apartment that it spilled out into the courtyard below. The students just wanted to build relationships with fellow neighbors.

228 ›› Pancake Breakfast

At Northern Wisconsin, a Catalytic campus, students offered a free pancake breakfast at Marathon along with free literature. The event provided great exposure by saturating the entire campus. Serving the pancakes was good PR for Campus Crusade and they got a positive response.

QUESTIONNAIRES››

229 ›› Leadership Interview

Formerly at Texas Christian University, a female Campus Crusade staff member told how she would call the president of each sorority and say, "Hi, I'm new to campus. I would like to learn more about your sorority. Can we meet sometime?" Using 13 questions, the staff member found ways she could provide a resource for the sorority. If the president described unity as a problem, then she would respond and say, "Hey, I have a talk on unity. I would love to come down and speak." Let the Greeks know you can be a resource for them, and make yourself available to the Greek leaders.

This same approach can be used for the dorms. The same female Crusade staff made herself available to the RAs. She went to RA directors and handed them a brochure showing a list of programs she could do for them. RAs are scrambling for someone to help them fulfill their program requirements.

Howard University

NEWSPAPER OUTREACH

BY WILLIAM GRIFFIN

❝Our desire is to understand their worldview so that we're able to communicate the gospel more effectively.❞

Our desire is to see what students are talking about on campus and use that as an entry point to share the gospel. Jesus often did the same by using analogies from the culture that people understood.

Many students read the campus newspaper and there is usually a 'buzz' about some controversial article that was written. For example, recently a professor was accused of making college women pose in a magazine. We look for a general theme, in this case, what is moral? We take that opportunity to enter into dialogue with the student by providing a definition of the term moral from a 'universally accepted' resource, such as Webster's dictionary. If they agree with that definition, we begin a simple four-part questionnaire.

First, we craft a question such as, "Are you aware of the 'behavior' that was mentioned in the school newspaper?"

Second, we ask about their values in light of the behavior just mentioned.

Third, we ask, "What beliefs support their values?"

Fourth, we ask, "Where do their beliefs come from?"

Then, we transition by talking about what the Bible says about morality. We ask, "Would you mind hearing a brief presentation about being a true moral person?"

Our questionnaire is based on the "Onion Model" by Dr. Lloyd Kwast, which talks about peeling back the layers to discover a person's worldview. The worldview a person holds can change their perception of the gospel message. Our desire is to understand their worldview so that we're able to communicate the gospel more effectively. *

231 》》 Local Bagel Shop

Campus Crusade at Colorado State University mailed surveys to students. Students had to send the survey back in order to receive a free bagel coupon (donated from a local bagel shop).

232 》》 Smoking Questionnaire

Cincinnati Metro came up with a smoking questionnaire, used to approach smokers gathered for a "smoke break." The survey included questions like why they smoked and how many cigarettes they smoked. The last question would turn the topic toward spiritual issues. One staff member commented, "It's great because we found that most students don't like the fact that they smoke. So the survey created a need in them."

233 》》 Posting Results In Campus Newspaper

To assess the spiritual climate on their campus, students at Ohio University surveyed 5,000 students in one week. Then a week before "Faith Week," the college newspaper wrote an article posting the results of the survey.

234 》》 Pencils Attached to Surveys

At Southwest Missouri State, students filled out Campus Crusade surveys that registered them to win a $200 gift certificate to the mall. Pencils were attached to every survey to prevent students from having to wait in line. The winner for the gift certificate was announced at the weekly meeting. Other times during the year, Campus Crusade staff members reward students who complete a 15-minute survey with a $2 gift certificate to a local ice-cream shop.

235 》》 100 Conversations

At Dartmouth College, Campus Crusade led a two-week outreach called "100 Conversations." The outreach was a simple challenge for the students to initiate with their peers and request a 45-minute, 12-question, spiritual perspective and interview with them. The interview discusses topics such as religious background, impressions of Christians, and the relevancy of God to deep needs.

236 》》 Four-Question Men's Survey

At Boise State, one staff member designed a four-question survey just for men. The idea is not to rush through each question, but to engage in dialogue.

1. What's your definition of a man?

2. Why is it that males lead in all areas of negative social behavior?" Between 80-90% of all crime is male related: drunk driving, domestic violence, divorce. The idea of the second question is to get the student thinking about sin.

3. Do you think it is the responsibility for the man to initiate spiritual leadership with their wives or girlfriends?

4. If so, then what does this spiritual leadership look like?

If the timing is right, you can transition with this, "Another thing I share with people is a little booklet that explains the first steps of being the spiritual leader you were meant to be."

Note: Rick prefers to use the *Four Spiritual Laws* booklet.

237 ›› Freshmen Interviews

Each year, Campus Crusade receives the freshmen list from Virginia Tech administration. Campus Crusade sends out a letter (approved by the university) to invite every freshman to complete a 12-question interview. Someone from Campus Crusade then sets up an appointment for the interview. Of the 12 questions, the last four are spiritually related. "We just listen and try to set up a second appointment to talk about the gospel," says a staff member. For the last question, one might add, "We would love to talk more. Would you be willing to hear more about a relationship with God?"

238 ›› War Survey

At Western Kentucky, one student developed a War Survey to find out what students were thinking about the war. The survey had questions like, "What do you think of it?" "Does your religious faith cause you to think a certain way about the war?" "President Bush is known as a Christian. What do you think of that?"

239 ›› Using the Video Camera

At Arizona State, students have been taking a video camera on campus and grabbing people's opinions on tape. They ask deeper questions like: "What do you think truth is?" or "Do you think it's important to be tolerant?" or "What do you think of a person who thinks they have a monopoly on truth?" Students have taken their video camera to class, in their resident halls and to sports teams.

240 ›› Build a basketball hoop

At Cal State, Fresno, students built a basketball hoop during March Madness. They had a contest on who could make the most shots in 30 seconds. But to enter the contest, students were required to fill out surveys. This was an effective way to gather students. Gift certificates were given out as prizes. One year, they had a bike donated by a local bike shop.

241 ›› Know your students

Los Angeles is approaching a Latino population of 50 percent and it's beginning to show on campuses. Students living in LA have a high respect for God; they just need to hear the gospel. FSKs and initiative evangelism are accepted well in LA. One staff member shares, "A table and FSK have been highly effective. The more you mix giveaways with questionnaires, the better."

242 ›› Online Questionnaire

At UC Davis, Campus Crusade asked students to visit their Web site and enter an online questionnaire in order to win a TV, DVD, or a Playstation. They also gave away a few Playstations in the dorms to draw students to their table.

243 ›› When do you meet?

One student in the Milwaukee Metro area tallied all the surveys taken from the FSKs and put them into percentage forms. With the percentages on one side and the time for the weekly meeting on the other side, students handed cards out around campus. This way, the survey results were published and put to use, rather than just serving as a deceptive cover for creating contacts. "It was a great way to approach people," shares one staff member.

244 >> Sending a Faculty Letter

At the University of South Dakota, the faculty advisor for Campus Crusade writes a letter on behalf of Campus Crusade to the students. The advisor offers Campus Crusade as a resource for developing that part of life that may be neglected-the spiritual side. EveryStudent.com is also printed on the letter. Campus Crusade follows up the letter by calling students, asking them to complete a survey. Sending a faculty letter helps the faculty advisor to be more involved.

SERVICE EVANGELISM

245 >> Side by Side

Cal State in Fresno is inviting other clubs to help in community outreach events like offering a free car wash or taking food to a local rescue mission. Students have a ton of ideas as they brainstorm ways to expand on this theme. As students from other clubs work side by side with the Campus Crusade students, they build relationships and have opportunities to share the gospel. They have conducted a free car wash for students in the dorms. They also have organized a day to skip lunch and take food to a rescue mission.

246 >> Designated Drivers

James Madison University is taking a new approach to saving the lost. They are literally saving lives by offering to drive people home from parties. Instead of judging the drinking student, these Christian students are seeking ways to serve them and show them the love of Christ. Frequently they are asked, "Why are you doing this?"

247 >> 52-point Car Inspections

Not many college students know much about their cars; they just assume it will get them from point A to point B. Many times normal maintenance and upkeep can be sacrificed when there is a lack of money or time. Michigan Tech worked with local sponsors like Wal-Mart, Napa, and the Student Government to provide free 52-point car inspections, car washes, and even doing some minor repairs. This happened twice this year, the week before Thanksgiving and the last week before summer. Last time, close to 100 students brought their cars.

248 >> Spring Break II

Two weeks following spring break, the ministry at Michigan Tech dedicates a week of service on campus. Each day, the students minister to the campus in a different way. Each Bible study chooses a creative idea for their day and the whole group follows. Opportunities for servant evangelism abound within this week.

249 >> Ministry Even During FINALS!

How many times do students forget their "blue book" or that all-important #2 pencil? More times than can be counted. The University of New Mexico has risen to serve this tangible need of students. Along with the felt need of pencils and test booklets, hot chocolate was offered to the students. An evangelistic article was thrown into the mix by being enclosed in the test booklet.

250 >> You Want Me to Clean the Frat House?

Certainly sounds both scary and faith stretching. Columbus Metro cleaned fraternity houses and dorms as a part of their servant evangelism projects.

*Bonus!

We found 36 more ideas that were only printed in your copy of the book. Enjoy!

251›› Serving With the Campus

Often times a local campus will have service projects ready and waiting for excited student volunteers. The University of New Mexico helped clean up a Habitat for Humanity home. This is a great way for students to get their feet wet in service projects without the pressure to be creative. An added bonus is interacting with students on campus who share a concern for service and may not perceive Christians as caring for practical things. This could be a first step in showing the already concerned student the path to a greater way to care.

252›› U B Kind

Buffalo University hosted a U B Kind week and openly challenged the student body to do 10,000 acts of kindness in one week. The students could sign their acts of kindness on a banner or post to a Web site.

253›› Gifts of Love

Syracuse has garnered the excitement of their students by pushing service projects. They have done multitudes ranging from free cookies and coffee in the lounge at midnight, to bringing sports drinks to the gym, each time asking for prayer needs.

254›› Midnight Dogs

Oregon State decided to reach out to the Greek system when they were available and have a BBQ for them. Students can be busy all day, but one time they're not is midnight.

That's when they hosted the Hot Dog BBQ. The secret's not the sauce, but the time.

255›› Relaxing With Mr. Happy

Towson did a stress relief station. They gave back massages and supplied cookies, fruit, and juice as students left their classes.

256›› Garbage Ministry

Art schools can be very hostile, and one way Maryland Institute and College of Art is working to break down those hostilities and stereotypes is through the garbage ministry. Every week students knock on doors and ask to pick up their tras. They explain who they are and why they are doing it. Their goals are to serve the community and get to know the students.

257›› Pre-Pay Coffees

A Rutgers women's study collected money from each student and pre-purchased coffees for the incoming customers. When the customers wondered why the coffee was free, they were directed where the women were hanging out. When thanked for the coffee, they responded, "This is free because of what Jesus did on the cross for us. In essence, the coffee was paid in the same way Jesus paid for your sins." The coffee shop was owned by Christians who defrayed some of the costs themselves as a way to help the outreach.

258›› Exam Time Love

U. Virginia Impact has given out bags of candy and encouragement to students preparing for tests at midnight in the libraries. It was a great way of showing love to the student body.

259》 "It's Free. Coming Soon." Campaign

Eastern Kentucky provided free stuff for people all over campus for a week. They hyped it up with ads in the paper, "Its free. Coming Soon." The week of free stuff included carwashes, free cokes at Greek meetings, free coins in the laundry room. In addition, people's trash was taken out. High profile service can be used as a way to bridge to the gospel. Marshall University also used this campaign and handed out donated sub sandwiches, brownies, and freshman move in service.

260》 K-Ville Hot Chocolates

Students stand in line for hours the night before Duke home games for the chance at tickets. Duke decided to serve hot chocolate to the students waiting in line. They also gave out free Mugs that say "K-Ville" ("K" for head coach Mike Krzyzewski) with the year. Coach K always comes out to speak and even buys all the students pizza.

261》 Finals Survival Kits, a new Spin on FSK.

Cal Poly, San Luis began personally handing out Finals Survivor Kits – a clever take on the FSK concept. The bag includes testing supplies like #2 pencils, blue books, scan-trons, as well as a snack and a note of encouragement.

262》 Can you handle it?

Bathroom Service? That's right, weekend bathroom service in a dorm. That's crazy talk! Humboldt is doing just that. Sunday afternoons, students clean the dorm bathrooms. Warning: Thick Rubber gloves are a must!

263》 Starbucks Giveaway

Sometimes students desire a quality product, generic doesn't communicate quite the same. Humboldt gave away fresh Starbucks coffee brewed within sight of the dorms. This went hand in hand with a freshman move in project. This really ministered to the parents as well as the incoming freshmen.

264》 Free Henna Tattoos

Cal State Fullerton had a tattoo artist giving free Henna Tattoos. They also had professional upper back massages free on the quad. Both took place by the Campus Crusade table.

SPEAKERS

265》 A Texas Sized Millionaires Forum

Southern Methodist University used the Millionaires Forum to share he gospel with the whole Cox Business School. The millionaires were invited to speak in 16 different classrooms and they were able to share the gospel in every classroom. The millionaires went in pairs; one shared his story for 10 minutes while the other answered questions afterwards. The professors enjoyed their guests and some even gave them the whole class time. The ministry is hoping to do the same next year utilizing local business people from Dallas.

266 ›› Hearing From a Millionaire

Western Oregon University offered the Millionaires Forum. Randy Conrad, founder of classmates.com and co-owner of the Phoenix Suns, shared how the Lord can help a person succeed. He also shared the gospel and his testimony. Other speakers joined Randy to talk about how God helped them develop proper business ethics.

267 ›› Veritas Forum

Veritas Forum week at Cal Poly at San Luis Obispo featured speakers tasked with challenging the thinking of students. Two of the topics covered were "Evidence for Faith" and "Jesus verses Bruce Lee." Churches partnered with the forum and local pastors hosted a number of the seminars. The forum took place in the plaza area of the student union and the ministry offered coffee and couches with music playing in the background.

268 ›› A Moody Partnership

Chicago Metro has a partnership with the Moody Church to host outreaches each month. A speaker is brought in on various topics. In Chicago there are many professors from Christian seminaries, so the metro team can rotate from school to school to bring in speakers. At one of the outreaches, a professor talked about gay lifestyles and relationships.

269 ›› The Keyes to Faith

Former presidential candidate, Dr. Allen Keyes spoke on the topic of "Faith in the Public Arena" at Wayne State University. Campus Crusade hosted the event in partnership with the Student Alumni, Inter Varsity and Chi Alpha.

270 ›› 3,200 Curious about Existence of God

Campus Crusade at Indiana University brought in Dr. William Lang Craig to debate the existence of God. Craig debated against a leading atheist from Texas University. More than 3,200 students attended and hundreds more had to be turned away. The staff team at IU used comment cards to reconnect with students after the event.

271 ›› Greg Ganssle

Ohio University's Campus Crusade enlisted the speaking services of Greg Ganssle. Greg has been on staff with Campus Crusade for 22 years and has a Ph.D in philosophy. Greg speaks on a variety of topics. At Ohio he spoke on the problem of evil.

272 ›› 911 Survivor

At Purdue, Campus Crusade brought in Sujo John to speak. Sujo survived the September 11th attacks on the World Trade Center and gave his testimony to the students.

273 ›› Boston Metro Brings in Speakers

The ministry in Boston brought in three speakers recently. Peter Kreeft, a Boston College philosopher uses a keyhole analogy to describe how we are all looking for the perfect key. Kreeft speaks on the twelve ways that Christianity fits that keyhole. At least 1/4 of the audience were non-Christians and Kreeft received a standing ovation. The other speakers were Fritz Schaefer, a University of Georgia chemist, and Paul Nelson, who spoke on Intelligent Design.

Get the Word
out on campus

You can add your location information right on the ad.

Download free posters and
more at www.ESCmedia.org

"Bob and his team mobilized the students to pray and God answered.

274
An Enthusiastic Endorsement
Coumbus Metro
BY NICK CORROVA

The most fruitful ministry experience the Columbus Metro Team saw this year was with Bob Boyd Ministries. Bob, an evangelist, shared the gospel at five college campuses during a six-day campaign and spoke to more than 950 students--plus athletic teams, fraternities, sororities, and faculty members. About 289 people indicated decisions for Christ!

"Over the last few years," said staff member Nick Corrova, "I have heard a lot about the 'lack of effectiveness' with program evangelism. However, I have never come close to seeing our Lord produce so much fruit in such a short time as He did in this outreach. The response was way beyond our expectations."

Bob and his team mobilized the students to pray and God answered. "Our team and the students are currently swamped with all of the follow-up," says Nick. "What a great problem to have!" ✻

275›› Seven-foot-tall Laker shares faith

Ex-professional basketball player Bay Forest spoke at Southern Oregon University. The ministry brought him in to provide an evangelistic talk at their weekly meeting. Forest is 7 feet tall and played for the Los Angeles Lakers in the 1970's. Students enjoyed him and the event helped establish a sense on campus that Campus Crusade's weekly meeting was a safe place to come and check out Christianity.

276›› Norman Geisler at Easter

At Easter the ministry at Indiana University of Pennsylvania joined with other Christian groups to bring in Norman Geisler. During the event, a survey entitled "Resurrection: History

MORE SPEAKERS ››

of Myth?" was given to the students. Bible studies were also available for the students.

277 》》 Princeton's Faculty Appreciation Luncheon

Campus Crusade students at Princeton host a Faculty Appreciation Luncheon where students invite one of their professors. Each student shared for 15 seconds about his or her professor. Walter Bradley spoke on the scientific evidence for the existence of God. Bradley also shared his testimony with the theme of moving beyond success to significance.

278 》》 Juggler Shares Christ

Campus Crusade at Towson University brought in a world-class juggler who is an alum of Towson. The event was held in the hub of campus and the juggler did a show involving the audience. First he shared his story and then networked the crowd. At the end, the juggler spoke briefly about his faith and introduced CRU. Staff gave away Testimony CD's and were able to do follow-up after that.

279 》》 Humor Bridge

Clemson University utilized two staff from the MidSouth regional office to do a comedy show touching on issues of student life. Rhet McGlaughlin and Link Neal were the emcees for the Greensboro Christmas Conference. Rhet and Link used college-related issues to springboard to spiritual issues. The event opened up a lot of opportunities to open spiritual conversations.

280 》》 Song of Solomon

The ministry at East Tennessee State University helped to sponsor Tommy Nelson's Song of Solomon conference. More than 1,000 students attended.

281 》》 Faith and Scholarship Forum

Jacksonville Metro teamed up with a former staff member to do the "Faith and Scholarship Forum" with students and faculty. The former staff is now a pastor at East Side Community Church. During part of the forum a heart surgeon from Portland came in to give a talk on intelligent design.

282 》》 Rittenhouse Speaks to 40% Of Student Body

The ministry brought Jon Rittenhouse in to the University of Redlands in Los Angeles. Rittenhouse debated the head of the philosophy department on the topic of "Does God Exist?" Students organized the entire event and 40% of the student body attended the debate.

283 》》 Surfing Dude

Students at UC Santa Barbara used the ocean to point people to Jesus. "Changes", a surfing video, was shown on campus. Afterward, a pro surfer spoke to the students.

284 》》 Firefighters for Christ

Captain John Smith, director of Firefighters for Christ, spoke at the University of Southern California. Smith is a strong believer and the event brought about a huge response from the students.

285 》》 Leaders Challenged by Coors

Milwaukee Metro had Adolf Coors speak to faculty and student leaders during a luncheon. Coors shared how he reached the peak of success and lost everything. Coors' talk was challenging to the leaders and his story was beneficial for Greek students, athletic teams and dorm leaders.

286 >> "Mind Seige" in South Dakota

David Noble, author of "Mind Seige" with Tim LaHaye, spoke at the University of South Dakota. Noble used his book to address the college culture in general. Additionally, he gave away many free books and paid for an ad in the school paper.

IDEAS FOR THE FUTURE >>

We would like to have a "Rites of Passage" for freshmen men. We would meet in focus groups in the dorms and discuss what it means to be a man. (Tennessee State University – IMPACT)

We would like to use the FSK laundry bags separately and do a Laundry Outreach by placing a small box of detergent in the bag along with an insert advertising the campus web site. (North Carolina State)

We would like to bring in the dean of philosophy from Notre Dame, who is a believing Catholic, to talk with our students and faculty. (North Carolina State)

We would like to have a "Greek House Clean Up" on Saturday mornings. We would serve the fraternities by cleaning their houses. (Colorado State University)

We would like to bring in JoePix for tailgating. (Michigan State)

We would like to host book clubs where students discuss various books with spiritual undertones. (Toledo)

We would like to meet on Saturdays for mountain biking. All the students could meet somewhere and bring their friends. We would then stop and have lunch together. (U of Montana)

We would like to train our students to write letters to editors. (Atlanta Metro)

We would like to reach the 200 students who will run for next year's leadership positions on campus. We would talk with them, listen to them, hear their story, and give them a CD of student testimonies. (Berkeley)

We would like to bring the Alpha Course to our campus. We heard of a campus ministry that used the program and saw students come to Christ. (Cal State, Chico)

We would like to serve the students by changing the oil in their cars. The event would be held in the dorm parking lot. (Humboldt)

We would like to cancel the weekly meeting for one week and have our students invite their friends to a dinner held in their apartments. (San Diego)

We would like to have students bring their book receipts to the weekly meeting and have a drawing where the winner gets their books paid for. (Dickinson State)

Every Student .com

It's easy.
Now you can present the gospel to every student on campus easily, and in a way that's comfortable for others to consider God. Just send them to a Web site, EveryStudent.com. It's right there in their dorm room, apartment, fraternity/ sorority, every hour, every day. And it's free.

Student leaders love it.
One student leader emailed saying: "I just wanted to say that this website is awesome. You guys deliver truth so clearly to a post modern generation without compromising anything. I can't wait to send this website info to friends who are not Christians."

> **I cannot get this God stuff out of my head. I wonder if your God exists if he even cares about me.**

Another wrote: "This website is awesome-- the perfect way to speak God's word without threats."

Covers lots of topics.

Such as: sex and relationships, astrology, drinking, various religions, purpose in life, eating disorders, stress, existence of God, feminism, racial issues, why Jesus, and more. Every page is evangelistic, and most students who check out the site stay long enough to read several articles. They're not just clicking around and gone. In the 2002-2003 school year, more than 2,600 students said they received Christ while on the site.

Students can email a question.

The anonymity of EveryStudent.com makes it easy for students to ask what they'd really like to know. They can email a question and receive a personal email response.

"I cannot get this God stuff out of my head. I wonder if your God exists if he even cares about me. I've done some pretty stupid stuff in my life and I wonder if there really is this good God out there if he would even look my way. My thoughts are that he would look my way in disdain and complete and utter disappointment. I wouldn't fit in with you Christians at all. I enjoy the college life way too much. But thoughts about whether or not there is a God won't go away. I really would like for them to but they are constantly on my mind."

It's easy to refer to in conversations.

In personal evangelism, Christian students can go to the site for quick answers to tough questions, and it's easy to say to others: "Great question. There's a Web site that covers that question really well...EveryStudent.com."

Sending students to EveryStudent.com is easy and inexpensive.

There's no drain on your campus budget. All posters, cards, buddy icons for IM and such are free, at www.ESCmedia.org. Making the site known on campus is fun and easy. As one Christian student put it: "We want to reach every student on campus. It really couldn't get any easier than EveryStudent.com."

TOP FIVE
EVANGELISM RESOURCES FROM IVP

TOP FIVE
EVANGELISM RESOURCES

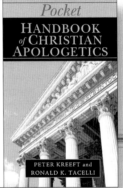

OUT OF THE SALTSHAKER
Rebecca Manley Pippert draws on over 25 years of experience sharing the gospel in this classic that can help you make evangelism a way of life.
0-8308-**2220**-8, $13.00

JESUS WITH DIRTY FEET
Don Everts introduces the curious and skeptical to the Jesus who partied, cooked breakfast, changed the world and had dirty feet.
0-8308-**2206**-2, $5.00

EVANGELISM OUTSIDE THE BOX
Rick Richardson offers new ways to tell the old, old story and reach a postmodern generation.
0-8308-**2276**-3, $11.00

HOW TO GIVE AWAY YOUR FAITH
Marie Little has revised this edition of Paul Little's time-tested guide that helps you face your evangelism fears and find effective and biblical ways to overcome them.
0-8308-**1217**-2, $12.00

POCKET HANDBOOK OF CHRISTIAN APOLOGETICS
Peter Kreeft and Ronald K. Tacelli summarize the foremost arguments for major Christian teachings and offer compelling responses to common arguments put forward against Christianity.
0-8308-**2702**-1, $7.00

GET 30% OFF for personal or give-away use, and 20% off for resale to students when you order from InterVarsity Press and identify yourself as CCC staff. SRC: 611-16

ivp INTERVARSITY PRESS   CALL (630.734.4321) TO ORDER TODAY

CAPT. JEFF STRUECKER

Description: CPT Jeff Struecker was a Ranger sergeant in Mogadishu, Somalia in the summer of 1993. As described in the book and movie Black Hawk Down, it was in his Humvee that the first American was killed by enemy fire in Somalia. Upon returning to the air base, he learned he would have to go back into the city to help rescue the men from the fallen Black Hawk. Struecker continues serving his nation and God as a chaplain in the 82nd Airborne. Through a compelling 45-minute presentation, Struecker shares how his faith in God gave him the courage to face his own death.

Contact: The Military Ministry at 757-247-7502. They are taking names and numbers while Struecker is deployed.

STACEY KOLE
www.staceykole.com
Description: Stacey Kole won the title Miss Arizona USA 1998 and placed sixth in the nation at the nationally televised Miss USA Pageant. After personally experiencing an eating disorder, Stacey has devoted the past ten years to serving as an advocate for eating disorder education and prevention. She is a frequent speaker to colleges, high schools and women's groups. Stacey Kole will visit your campus to speak on eating disorders, to share her personal experience with pageants and the beauty culture, and how she found healing through a personal relationship with God. A 40-55 minute event to sororities, dorms, and other campus groups is scheduled and promoted. The gospel is shared within the context of Stacey's personal testimony. Comment cards are then distributed for the purpose of follow-up.

Contact: skole@cox.net or call 480-839-5593

SUHO JOHN
www.SujoJohn.com
Description: Sujo John, a New Yorker, was on the 81st floor of Tower I when the first airliner exploded into flames just two floors above his office. His wife's office was in Tower II. His heart was heavy as he descended the steps wondering if he would live

to see their unborn child or his wife ever again. Sujo shares his incredible story and challenges his audience with the single question, "Do you know where you are going?"

Contact: SujoJ@hotmail.com
Video: www.sujoatpurdue.com

DARRELL SCOTT
www.columbineredemption.com
Description: Darrell Scott is the father of Rachel Joy Scott, a victim of the Columbine High School massacre. His son, Craig, was in the library that day and watched as 10 of his classmates were gunned down. Darrell has partnered with Campus Crusade to take Rachel's story of love for God and others to college students around the country. Darrell has spoken at more than 65 campuses.

Contact Info: Dana Ashley at 615.370.4700 x233 or email at Dana@AmbassadorAgency.com

ANDRE KOLE
www.andrekole.org
Description: The first part of Andre's performance consists of illusions that are guaranteed to delight and astound all. It's full of wholesome family entertainment. During the second part of the performance, as Andre tells how he came to realize his need for Christ, he shares how each person can experience a personal relationship with God through Jesus Christ.

Contact: scheduling@andrekole.org or call 480/ 968-8625.

THE MILLIONAIRE'S FORUM
The purpose of the Millionaire's Forum is to bring highly successful business professionals together to share the gospel through the story of Christ's work in their lives and businesses successes. The Forum is built around a sumptuous invitation-only dinner for the top 25 non-Christian student leaders. The event takes advantage of other on-campus speaking venues such as business related classes, a luncheon with the top Christian student leaders, meetings with key university leadership, fraternities and sororities, and

the weekly meeting. For those campuses that qualify, the expenses for the Forum and related events are completely paid for by the speaking team.

Contact: Tom Waller at 949.366.4003 or email at twaller@historyshandful.org

JON RITTENHOUSE

Description: Jon Rittenhouse has been on staff with Campus Crusade for Christ for 25 years working with college students. He has spoken on over 100 universities across the United States and in five foreign countries. John has a passion for training students to be more effective in evangelism and to be prepared to defend their faith using apologetics. His topics include: Is One True Religion Really Possible?, Is Truth Just A Matter of Opinion?, Does it Really Matter What We Believe?, Is Tolerance really Tolerant?, Is it Arrogant to say that Jesus is the Only Way?,The Occult: Doorway to the Supernatural or Dangerous Dabblings?,Spiritual Experience and Life after Death, Is Christianity really Credible?

Contact: Jon may be reached at (909) 864-4431 or at JonRit@aol.com

DAVE GEISLER
www.meeknessandtruth.org
Description: Dave is a former Crusade staff member and the son of the well-known Christian Apologist, Norm Geisler. Dave has recently developed a transferable evangelism model (The THINK Methodology) that has been proven helpful in reaching certain kinds of postmoderns. Dave has now taught this model on university campuses across the United States and many college ministries have already incorporated this methodology into their evangelism strategies. Dave's 15 years of college ministry experience, his heart for evangelism, and his training in apologetics has given him a wealth of resources to train students and staff in how to more effectively use apologetics in practical evangelism. Dave's ministry (Meekness and Truth Ministries) has made many of their teaching resources available for others to freely down load and use off their Internet site.

Contact: Dave may be reached at (512) 248-8658 or at dgeisler@meeknessandtruth.org

BOB BOYD
www.bobboyd.org
Description: Bob Boyd has been a National Collegiate Speaker for 17 years (12 on staff with Campus Crusade), and has presented Christ to hundreds of thousands of students on over 150 campuses. Bob and the Team specialize in: 1) firing up students for prayer and personal evangelism through single and multi-day retreats and conferences, and 2) impacting campuses through 3-5 day campus-wide evangelistic campaigns. Speaking topics include: How to Be the Leader You Were Meant to Be, How to Have a Great Love Life, God: Fact, or Fantasy?

Contact: Stephen Doyle at 757-624-9001, or email at sdoyle@bobboyd.org

JOE WHITE
http://www.whatsafterdark.com
"After Dark" features noted author and speaker Joe White as he takes on the role of the Roman cross builder, examining the crucifixion through the eyes of those who witnessed it personally. Musical guests who have strong college followings, such as By The Tree, perform and help to reach individuals to make decisions for Christ.

Contact: Don at donford@whatsafterdark.com

BRANDON SLAY
www.BrandonSlay.com
www.GreaterGold.com
Description: Brandon Slay won the 2000 Olympic Gold Medal in Freestyle Wrestling in Sydney, Australia. He graduated from the University of Pennsylvania. For many years he attempted to accomplish his wrestling dreams without God, and he only got so far. He realized his life was empty and only God could bless the desires of his heart. Brandon has started an organization called Greater Gold, which teaches students there is a "New Way to Win" and a "New Way to Live" through a personal relationship with Jesus Christ. Brandon travels speaking to schools about becoming a success. He also gives a great abstinence message.

Contact: Evan Morganstein at 919-363-5105 or mail at pmgevan@earthlink.net

AMBASSADOR SPEAKERS BUREAU
www.AmbassadorAgency.com

Description: Ambassador Speakers Bureau is the leading provider of more than 100 Christian speakers in the United States. Their purpose is to honor Jesus Christ by assisting Christian leaders who understand what it means to live and think informed by a Biblical world-view. Speakers include: Kirk Cameron, Danya Curry, Os Guiness, Lisa Beamer.

Contact: 615.370.4700 or email info@ambassador ragency.com

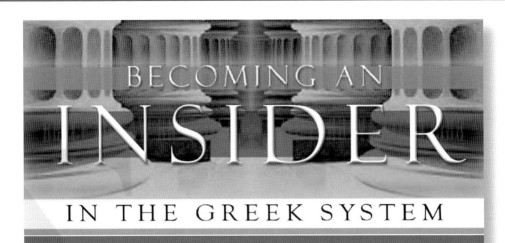

BECOMING AN INSIDER

IN THE GREEK SYSTEM

The goal of this book is to help you become an insider in the Greek system and then to ultimately work yourself out of a job in ministering within a fraternity or sorority. Our prayer is that regardless of what ministry you are associated with, this book will provide you with some basic principles that will give you confidence and make you more effective in ministering to Greeks in your chapter and on your whole campus.

a handbook for campus staff

ISAAC JENKINS & SCOTT SOMMER

For information about purchasing this book or finding other Greek ministry resources
email: Greek@uscm.org or call: Teila Higgins at 1.888.405.4222 ext.25

*RESOURCES

Resources & Phone Numbers

The 250, Evangelism Ideas for your Campus: To order call New Life Resources.

Greek Ministry handbooks: Contact Telia Higgins in the Southeast Regional Office at 1.888.405.4222

CD Journal: Rick James & Tim Henderson. Provides input on many ways to reach your campus. Email centerfield@uscm.org or visit http://centerfieldproductions.com.

The CoJourner Pack is a resource providing small group leaders with 20 discussion cards to guide students toward an intentional lifestyle of evangelism. Include a card in your small group as a training nugget to help students take another step in evangelism. To order call New Life Resources or visit www.campuscrusade.org.

Student/Greek planners: The planners were created in 1998 as an evangelistic tool to get your foot in the door by hosting a time management seminar and giving sharp Franklin Covey planners to each member. For more info: www.cccplanners.com. E-mail planners@uscm.org or call 1-888-405-4222 ext. 24 to order.

Freshmen Survival Kits: To order, visit "Tools" on the Staff Site.

QuEST: A Nationally Sponsored Research Project. Used as an outreach tool, the QuEST survey uncovers trends in the thoughts of college students. Go to the Evangelism: Tools: QuEST folder in the Resource Center to find updated training materials and the QuEST surveys. Please upload your QuEST results under "Tools" on the Staff Site. WSN Press: Campus Crusade resources available. Call New Life Resources.

Gilbert's Coaching Tips: A weekly email sent from one coach to another. Each week, Gilbert Kingsley offers new and fresh tools, resources, and strategies to use in your campus ministry. To be added to the list, email Yvonne.Rivera@uscm.org.

Student Evangelism Ideas: Evangelism ideas from the MidSouth Region can be found in the Resource Center in the Regional Info: MidSouth folder under "Student Evangelism Taskforce."

The Art of Conversation: Ryan McReynolds from the GPI Regional Office has written a great resource regarding the 'art' of guided conversations - how to ask good questions, how to dialogue with someone, etc. It is now available in the Evangelism: Equipping folder of the Resource Center.

NLTC for the 00's: Bruce Henderson has written new NLTC-like lessons on relating to non-Christians. based on "Finding Common Ground," by Tim Downs. These lessons are designed to help students learn how to relate to non-Christians in order to reach them. Find Bruce's notes in the Evangelism: Equipping folder of the Resource Center.

New Life Resources: 1.800.827.2788

Finding Common Ground: How to Communicate With Those Outside the Christian Community ... While We Still Can by Tim Downs.

Web sites

The Staff Site:
https://staff.campuscrusadeforchrist.com

The Campus Ministry Resource Center: A great place to visit when you don't want to reinvent the wheel or to share resources you like to use. Click "Resources" on the Staff Site.

Visit **www.EvangelismToolbox.org** to locate evangelism tools.

Visit **www.CampusStories.org** to find hundreds of stories and evangelism ideas from college campuses nationwide.

Visit **www.ServantEvangelism.com** to find hundreds of ways to lead servant evangelism on your campus.

MORE RESOURCES ››

Resources CONTINUED...

Visit **www.impactmovement.com** to see what God is doing among African American students.

Visit **www.destino.cc** to see what God is doing among Hispanic students.

Visit **www.epicmovement.com** to see what God is doing among Asian American students.

www.campuscrusadeforchrist.com - The public website for the US Campus Ministry.

www.ESCMedia.org: The place to get the goods for media campaigns to target your campus using EveryStudent.com. Get the word out and become visible on campus, using posters, newspaper ads and printed articles.

www.EveryStudent.com: An easy, inexpensive way to reach students with the gospel right where they are...on the Internet.

www.godsquad.com: God is raising up a network of student-led, staff-coached Campus Crusade for Christ ministries at colleges across the United States. This is where you find all the materials and strategies!

http://www.waymakers.org/freshprayer.html - FreshPrayer is a monthly prayer guide designed to help ordinary Christians pray with hope and biblical clarity for people they know who have yet to follow Christ. Every issue of FreshPrayer consists of a participant's guide and a leader's guide.

ACKNOWLEDGEMENTS

It takes many to pull together a good research project like this. First I'd like to thank all the campuses we interviewed for this project. Truly the most creative ideas originate from the field.

I'd like to thank Erik Segalini, editor for Worldwide Challenge, for editing the hundreds of ideas. It was a real pleasure to have him join our project. I'd also like to thank Mark Winz for lending his expertise and helping us understand the publication process. A special thanks to Greg Kriefall for taking time while in New York City to edit Keith's introductions.

John Trzcinski edited 15 of our featured articles. Thanks John for making them "well done" for our readers. I've enjoyed our times at Giovanni's while working on this project.

Every editor needs a writer like Lisa Larson. Lisa can write fast and write well. Making our May 14th deadline would have been impossible without her help.

Pat Schleper helped a friend see his vision become a reality. Pat offered much more than 12 hours of his time. Thanks so much Pat.

Daniela Byers interviewed all those campuses in the Midsouth, Greater Northwest, and some of the Great Plains. Daniela also contributed over 45 illustrations for this project.

Tanya Walker interviewed our friends up in the Northeast. It was fun to have her with us for a short while.

I always looked forward to seeing Matt Ely on Thursdays and Fridays. His humor gave lift to our team. Those unique Web sites he forwarded our way were a good distraction to the team.

I'd also like to thank Suzanne Dunn for her help. Suzanne interviewed the campuses in the Southeast during times when her sixteen-month old Natalie was napping.

Thank you Kim Sanwald for being a part of our team this year. I'm looking forward to having you join us next year.

Jeff Helms offered words of encouragement that gave me lift when I was down. I had many self-doubts throughout this project and sometimes it was hearing his words that pushed me through. Jeff helped interview and edit. Thanks Jeff for being available when we needed you.

Amanda Hitchock interviewed a lot of campuses, and edited many, many of those ideas. Amanda is a talented writer, but the quality I admire best in her is that she "gets the job done." Thanks for hanging in there Amanda.

A special thanks to Nathan Dunn for listening to the wild and crazy ideas I had and for believing in me to try a few of them. Nathan worked long and hard on the different evangelism modes. It was also Nathan's challenge that motivated the team to press on and complete the 170 marker. Nathan, thank you for contributing when I absolutely needed you to.

How many staff can say they worked on an evangelism project with Keith Davy? It has been a highlight to work with Keith, and a year I shall never forget. The LX Review would have never taken off without Keith and our partnership with Research and Development. We never would have arrived at our destination without Keith behind the wheel.

A special thanks to Brian Byers and Chris Anderson, our design team from the Innovation Center for Technology. Thank you for taking us to the finishing line.

Finally, we are ever so grateful for our Lord. We humbly offer this work to Him and pray that many would come to know Him personally as a result. To God be all the glory.

Larry Stephens
Project Coordinator
Campus Communications

*INDEX

*NOTES

(APPENDIX A)

(THE TWO-FIFTY)

the**250**

Evangelism Ideas For Your Campus

Over 250
EVANGELISM IDEAS

Over 170 college campuses
INTERVIEWED

And so much more!!!

To order additional copies of "The250" for your campus, or evangelism
team, call toll free 1.800.827.2788, or visit www.campuscrusade.org

Available Now. Everywhere.